HSE

Managing and working with asbestos

Control of Asbestos Regulations 2012

Approved Code of Practice and guidance

HSE Books

First published 2006
Second editon 2013

ISBN 978 0 7176 6618 8

Approved Code of Practice

This Code has been approved by the Health and Safety Executive, with the consent of the Secretary of State. It gives practical advice on how to comply with the law. If you follow the advice you will be doing enough to comply with the law in respect of those specific matters on which the Code gives advice. You may use alternative methods to those set out in the Code in order to comply with the law.

However, the Code has a special legal status. If you are prosecuted for breach of health and safety law, and it is proved that you did not follow the relevant provisions of the Code, you will need to show that you have complied with the law in some other way or a Court will find you at fault.

Guidance

This guidance is issued by the Health and Safety Executive. Following the guidance is not compulsory, unless specifically stated, and you are free to take other action. But if you do follow the guidance you will normally be doing enough to comply with the law. Health and safety inspectors seek to secure compliance with the law and may refer to this guidance.

Contents

Introduction

About this book

1 This publication contains the Control of Asbestos Regulations 2012, the Approved Code of Practice (ACOP) text and associated guidance. The Regulations place legal duties on employers responsible for licensable and non-licensable work with asbestos. They also place a specific duty to manage asbestos on the owners and/or those responsible for maintenance in non-domestic premises. The ACOP text and guidance provide practical advice on how to comply with those requirements. The format of this publication is designed to clearly distinguish between the Regulations, the ACOP text and the guidance.

2 The Control of Asbestos Regulations 2012 (the Regulations) set minimum standards for the protection of employees from risks related to exposure to asbestos. Employers should also take account of people not directly employed by them but who could be affected by the work being done on asbestos (including employees of other employers, people occupying buildings, members of the public etc).

3 The Regulations came into force on 6 April 2012, updating and replacing the previous 2006 version of the Regulations. The changes mean that certain types of non-licensable work with asbestos now have additional requirements on notification of work; designating areas where work on asbestos is being carried out; medical surveillance and record keeping. This publication applies to work which disturbs, or is likely to disturb asbestos, asbestos sampling and laboratory analysis.

Environmental issues

4 The Regulations deal only with health risks to people from asbestos. They do not address environmental issues. Further guidance on environmental considerations, including the clearing of asbestos-contaminated land is available from the following (see 'Further sources of advice'):

- the Environment Agency (EA) in England;
- the Scottish Environment Protection Agency (SEPA) in Scotland;
- Natural Resources Wales (NRW)/Cyfoeth Naturiol Cymru.

Consulting employees and/or safety representatives

5 Proper consultation with those who do the work, including all those who may be affected by the presence of asbestos in their workplace, is crucial in helping to raise awareness of the importance of health and safety. It can make a significant contribution to creating and maintaining a safe and healthy working environment and an effective health and safety culture. In turn, this can benefit business in making it more efficient by reducing the number of accidents and incidents of work-related ill health.

6 Employers must consult safety representatives appointed by recognised trade unions under the Safety Representatives and Safety Committees Regulations 1977. Employees who are not covered by such representatives must be consulted either directly or indirectly through elected representatives of employee safety under the Health and Safety (Consultation with Employees) Regulations 1996.[1]

About ACOPs

7 Approved Codes of Practice are approved by the HSE Board with the consent of the Secretary of State (see Appendix 1: Notice of Approval for details).

8 The ACOP describes preferred or recommended methods that can be used (or standards to be met) to comply with the Regulations and the duties imposed by the Health and Safety at Work etc Act (the HSW Act).[2] The accompanying guidance also provides advice on achieving compliance, or it may give information of a general nature, including explanation of the requirements of the law, more specific technical information or references to further sources of information.

9 The legal status of ACOP and guidance text is given on the copyright page.

Presentation

10 The ACOP text is set out in **bold** and the accompanying guidance in normal type, the text of the Regulations is in *italics*. Regulation 4, 'duty to manage asbestos in non-domestic premises' has a page border to help the reader identify the requirements under the regulation. This guidance was previously a stand-alone publication, L127, and has now been incorporated into this ACOP.

11 Each regulation is preceded by a short summary of the main duties imposed by that regulation and aims to help the reader navigate the document. This text has no 'status' (such as ACOP/guidance) and is for information only.

Regulation 1 Citation and commencement

Regulation 1

These Regulations may be cited as the Control of Asbestos Regulations 2012 and come into force on 6th April 2012.

Regulation 2 Interpretation

Summary

This regulation provides definition and interpretation of the terms used in the Regulations.

Regulation 2

(1) In these Regulations—

"adequate" means adequate having regard only to the nature and degree of exposure to asbestos, and "adequately" must be construed accordingly;

"appointed doctor" means a registered medical practitioner appointed for the time being in writing by the Executive for the purpose of these Regulations;

"approved" means approved for the time being in writing by the Executive;

"asbestos" means the following fibrous silicates—

- *(a) asbestos actinolite, CAS No 77536-66-4;*
- *(b) asbestos grunerite (amosite), CAS No 12172-73-5;*
- *(c) asbestos anthophyllite, CAS No 77536-67-5;*
- *(d) chrysotile, CAS No 12001-29-5 or CAS No 132207-32-0;*
- *(e) crocidolite, CAS No 12001-28-4; and*
- *(f) asbestos tremolite, CAS No 77536-68-6,*

and reference to "CAS" followed by a numerical sequence are references to CAS Registry Numbers assigned to chemicals by the Chemical Abstracts Service, a division of the American Chemical Society;

"asbestos cement" means a material which is predominantly a mixture of cement and chrysotile and which when in a dry state absorbs less than 30% water by weight;

"asbestos coating" means a surface coating which contains asbestos for fire protection, heat insulation or sound insulation but does not include textured decorative coatings;

"asbestos insulating board" (AIB) means any flat sheet, tile or building board consisting of a mixture of asbestos and other material except—

- *(a) asbestos cement; or*
- *(b) any article of bitumen, plastic, resin or rubber which contains asbestos, and the thermal or acoustic properties of the article are incidental to its main purpose;*

"asbestos insulation" means any material containing asbestos which is used for thermal, acoustic or other insulation purposes (including fire protection) except—

- *(a) asbestos cement, asbestos coating or asbestos insulating board; or*
- *(b) any article of bitumen, plastic, resin or rubber which contains asbestos and the thermal and acoustic properties of that article are incidental to its main purpose;*

Regulation 2

"the control limit" means a concentration of asbestos in the atmosphere when measured in accordance with the 1997 WHO recommended method, or by a method giving equivalent results to that method approved by the Executive, of 0.1 fibres per cubic centimetre of air averaged over a continuous period of 4 hours;

"control measure" means a measure taken to prevent or reduce exposure to asbestos (including the provision of systems of work and supervision, the cleaning of workplaces, premises, plant and equipment, and the provision and use of engineering controls and personal protective equipment);

"emergency services" include—

(a) police, fire, rescue and ambulance services;
(b) Her Majesty's Coastguard;

"employment medical adviser" means an employment medical adviser appointed under section 56 of the 1974 Act;

"enforcing authority" means the Executive, local authority or Office of Rail Regulation, determined in accordance with the provisions of the Health and Safety (Enforcing Authority) Regulations 1998 and the provisions of the Health and Safety (Enforcing Authority for Railways and Other Guided Transport Systems) Regulations 2006;

"ISO 17020" means European Standard EN ISO/IEC 17020, "General criteria for the operation of various types of bodies performing inspection" as revised or reissued from time to time and accepted by the Comité Européen de Normalisation Électrotechnique (CEN/CENELEC);

"ISO 17025" means European Standard EN ISO/IEC 17025, "General requirements for the competence of testing and calibration laboratories" as revised or reissued from time to time and accepted by the Comité Européen de Normalisation Électrotechnique (CEN/CENELEC);

"licensable work with asbestos" is work—

(a) where the exposure to asbestos of employees is not sporadic and of low intensity; or
(b) in relation to which the risk assessment cannot clearly demonstrate that the control limit will not be exceeded; or
(c) on asbestos coating; or
(d) on asbestos insulating board or asbestos insulation for which the risk assessment—
    (i) demonstrates that the work is not sporadic and of low intensity, or
    (ii) cannot clearly demonstrate that the control limit will not be exceeded, or
    (iii) demonstrates that the work is not short duration work;

"medical examination" includes any laboratory tests and X-rays that a relevant doctor may require;

"personal protective equipment" means all equipment (including clothing) which is intended to be worn or held by a person at work and which protects that person against one or more risks to that person's health, and any addition or accessory designed to meet that objective;

"relevant doctor" means an appointed doctor or an employment medical adviser. In

Regulation 2

relation to work with asbestos which is not licensable work with asbestos and is not exempted by regulation 3(2) "relevant doctor" also includes an appropriate fully registered medical practitioner who holds a licence to practice;

"risk assessment" means the assessment of risk required by regulation 6(1)(a);

"textured decorative coatings" means decorative and textured finishes, such as paints and ceiling and wall plasters which are used to produce visual effects and which contain asbestos. These coatings are designed to be decorative and any thermal or acoustic properties are incidental to their purpose, and

"the 1997 WHO recommended method" means the publication "Determination of airborne fibre concentrations. A recommended method, by phase-contrast optical microscopy (membrane filter method)", WHO (World Health Organisation), Geneva 1997.

(2) A reference to work with asbestos in these Regulations includes—

(a) work which consists of the removal, repair or disturbance of asbestos or materials containing asbestos;
(b) work which is ancillary to such work; and
(c) supervision of such work and such ancillary work.

(3) For the purposes of these Regulations, work with asbestos is not "short duration work" if, in any seven day period—

(a) that work, including any ancillary work liable to disturb asbestos, takes more than two hours; or
(b) any person carries out that work for more than one hour.

(4) For the purpose of these Regulations, no exposure to asbestos will be sporadic and of low intensity if the concentration of asbestos in the atmosphere, when measured in accordance with the 1997 WHO recommended method or by a method giving equivalent results to that method and approved by the Executive, exceeds or is liable to exceed the concentration approved in relation to a specified reference period for the purposes of this paragraph by the Executive.

(5) For the purposes of these Regulations, except in accordance with regulation 11(3) and (5), in determining whether an employee is exposed to asbestos or whether the extent of such exposure exceeds the control limit, no account must be taken of respiratory protective equipment which, for the time being, is being worn by that employee.

(6) In these Regulations the provisions of Appendix 7 to Annex XVII of the REACH Regulations, which determine the labelling requirements of articles containing asbestos, are reproduced in Schedule 2 (with minor changes reflecting the practical implementation of the requirements).

Guidance 2

Definition of 'asbestos'

12 'Asbestos' is the general term used for the fibrous silicates listed in regulation 2(1). Any mixture containing one or more of these fibrous silicates at more than trace amounts as defined in *Asbestos: The analysts' guide for sampling, analysis and clearance procedures (The analysts' guide)*[3] is within the definition. For any work covered by the Regulations, 'asbestos' also includes asbestos-containing materials (ACMs), containing any of these fibrous silicates or mixtures of them. Three main types of asbestos were commonly used:

Guidance 2

- crocidolite (commonly known as blue asbestos);
- amosite (commonly known as brown asbestos);
- chrysotile (commonly known as white asbestos).

13 Debris containing asbestos is also covered by the Regulations. If the debris contains raw asbestos, asbestos insulation, asbestos coating or asbestos insulating board (AIB), even where it is not fulfilling its original purpose, ie the asbestos materials may no longer be coating or insulating anything, a licensed asbestos contractor is required to carry out the work, unless it does not meet the conditions in the definition of licensable work in regulation 2(1).

Asbestos cement

14 Asbestos cement is mainly a mixture of chrysotile and cement, moulded and compressed to produce a range of asbestos products such as profiled roofing sheets and sidings, flat sheets, gutters, drainpipes, pressure pipes and flues.

15 Asbestos cement was widely used on the exterior of buildings and for drainage products, as it is weatherproof and waterproof and will absorb less water (<30%) than asbestos insulation or AIB (≥30%). Amosite and/or crocidolite asbestos have also been used in asbestos cement and may sometimes be present along with the chrysotile, but in smaller quantities.

16 As the asbestos fibres are mostly firmly bound into the cement matrix and not readily made airborne, work with asbestos cement does not pose the same risks as work with asbestos insulation, AIB and sprayed asbestos coatings. So, almost all work involving asbestos cement will not be licensable. However, there may be exceptional circumstances where asbestos cement has been so badly damaged and broken up that the work may become licensable. In these rare cases, a risk assessment will be required to determine if a licence is required.

Identifying asbestos cement products

17 A competent, experienced surveyor will normally be able to visually identify most asbestos cement products. But, if visual identification is inconclusive, analysis will be needed to establish the asbestos type(s). If, after analysis of the asbestos types, there is still doubt about whether a material is an asbestos cement product, a water absorption measurement will be needed, following the methodology set out at www.hse.gov.uk/asbestos/essentials/cement.htm to decide whether the material is asbestos cement.

18 Asbestos analysis laboratories should be able to do this test. A list of laboratories is available from the United Kingdom Accreditation Service (UKAS), see 'Further sources of advice'.

Textured decorative coatings

19 Textured decorative coatings containing asbestos are thin decorative and textured finishes, such as paints and ceiling plasters, used to produce visual effects. These coatings are designed to be decorative and any thermal or acoustic properties are incidental to their purpose. The proportion of asbestos in such coatings is normally between 2–5% chrysotile.

20 Work with textured decorative coatings will not normally be licensable work, as work with this material will usually not meet the conditions in the definition of licensable work in regulation 2(1).

Guidance 2

21 The term textured 'coating' does not apply to the base material the coating is applied to, even if that base material contains asbestos. (The base material may, however, fall within the definition of asbestos insulation or AIB.)

Asbestos insulating board (AIB)

22 AIB is a lightly compressed board made from asbestos fibre and hydrated Portland cement or calcium silicate with other filler materials. AIB is covered by the definition in regulation 2(1), whether or not the board is used for insulation. For instance, this definition still applies to AIB when its main purpose is structural, eg as a wall partition. Asbestos wallboard (a more compressed variety of AIB) also falls into this category.

Asbestos insulation

23 The definition of 'asbestos insulation' in regulation 2(1) describes ACMs, which were not in practice applied as coatings: those used for heat, sound, fire protection and other insulation purposes. This includes:

- preformed sections of pipe insulation;
- asbestos lagging and asbestos infill (asbestos used to fill the spaces between voids, applied between floors and packed around cables where they pass between floors);
- millboards (that have been used for insulation of electrical equipment and for thermal insulation).

Asbestos coating

24 'Asbestos coating' describes the various mixtures containing asbestos, widely used as surface coatings for fire protection purposes or as both heat and sound insulation. Most of these coatings were applied by spray but some were applied by hand.

25 Asbestos coating means the coating itself and not the base material it is applied to. However, in some cases the base material may also be an ACM (such as asbestos insulation or AIB).

ACOP 2

Sporadic and low intensity exposure

26 For the purposes of regulation 2(4), for exposure to be sporadic and of low intensity, the concentration of asbestos in the atmosphere should not exceed or be liable to exceed the concentration approved in relation to a specified reference period by the Health and Safety Executive.

27 This is 0.6 fibres per cubic centimetre (f/cm^3) in the air measured over a ten-minute period. Any exposure which exceeds or is liable to exceed this is not sporadic and of low intensity.

Guidance 2

28 The unit f/cm^3 is the same unit as f/ml. This ten-minute limit is sometimes called the short-term exposure limit or STEL. It refers to the highest level of concentration for any ten minute period of duration of the work. Note that this approved concentration for sporadic and low intensity exposure is not the same as the 'control limit' defined in regulation 2.

ACOP 2

Work with asbestos

29 'Work with asbestos' includes:

- work which removes, repairs or disturbs asbestos;
- work which is ancillary to such work (ancillary work);
- supervising the work referred to in the two bullet points above (supervisory work).

Licensable work

30 Certain types of work with ACMs can only be done by those who have been issued with a licence by HSE. This is work which meets the definition of 'licensable work with asbestos' in regulation 2(1). That is work:

- where worker exposure to asbestos is not sporadic and of low intensity (see paragraphs 26–27); or
- where the risk assessment cannot clearly demonstrate that the control limit (0.1 f/cm^3 airborne fibres averaged over a four-hour period) will not be exceeded; or
- on asbestos coating (surface coatings which contain asbestos for fire protection, heat insulation or sound insulation but not including textured decorative coatings); or
- on asbestos insulation or AIB where the risk assessment demonstrates that the work is not sporadic and of low intensity, the control limit will be exceeded and it is not short duration work.

31 Short duration means the total time spent by all workers working with these materials does not exceed two hours in a seven-day period, including time spent setting up, cleaning and clearing up, and no one person works for more than one hour in a seven-day period.

Guidance 2

Deciding if work is licensable

32 It is relatively easy to release asbestos fibres when working with asbestos insulation, asbestos coatings and AIB. In most cases, only those with a licence should carry out work with these materials. However, licensing will not apply to short-duration work where the risk assessment shows the work will only produce sporadic and low intensity exposure and will not exceed the control limit.

33 Employers need to consider whether the work meets the criteria set out in the definition of licensable work (see paragraph 30) and, if it does, a licence will be required. Licences are issued for a set period, during which the licence holder can carry out licensable work. A licence does not need to be issued for each individual work activity.

34 There is further information on applying for a licence from HSE in paragraphs 204–212.

35 Table 1 gives examples of licensable and non-licensable work.

Guidance 2

Table 1 Examples of licensable and non-licensable work

Work which requires a licence from HSE	Work which does not usually require a licence from HSE
Removing sprayed coatings (limpet asbestos) Removal or other work which may disturb pipe lagging Any work involving loose fill insulation Work on millboard Cleaning up significant quantities of loose/fine debris containing ACM dust (where the work is not sporadic and of low intensity, the control limit will be exceeded or it is not short duration work) Work on AIB, where the risk assessment indicates that it will not be of short duration	Small, short duration maintenance tasks where the control limits will not be exceeded Removing textured decorative coatings by any suitable dust-reducing method Cleaning up small quantities of loose/fine debris containing ACM dust (where the work is sporadic and of low intensity, the control limit will not be exceeded and it is short duration work) Work on asbestos cement products or other materials containing asbestos (such as paints, bitumen, resins, rubber, etc) where the fibres are bound in a matrix which prevents most of them being released (this includes, typically, aged/weathered AC) Work associated with collecting and analysing samples to identify the presence of asbestos

ACOP 2

Ancillary work

36 'Ancillary work' means work associated with the main work of repair, removal or disturbance of asbestos. Work carried out in an ancillary capacity requires a licence unless the main work (ie the removal, repair, disturbance activity) does not meet the conditions in the definition of licensable work.

37 'Ancillary work' includes maintenance work on equipment (eg class H vacuum cleaners (BS 8520-3:2009)[4] and air extraction equipment (including 'negative pressure' units) which involves contaminated (or potentially contaminated) parts of that equipment. 'Negative pressure' refers to air pressure in an enclosure being lower than the air outside it.

38 Ancillary work also includes putting up and taking down scaffolding, including any scaffolded frame, to provide access for licensable work, where it is foreseeable that the scaffolding activity is likely to disturb the asbestos.

Supervisory work

39 'Supervisory work' means work involving direct supervision over those removing, repairing or disturbing asbestos. This applies to supervisory work for both licensable and non-licensable activities.

Competence

40 Any reference in this document to competence, competent persons or competent employees is a reference to a person or employee who has received adequate information, instruction and training for the task being

ACOP 2

done and can demonstrate an adequate and up-to-date understanding of the work, required control measures and appropriate law. They must also have enough experience to apply this knowledge effectively.

Regulation 3 Application of these Regulations

Summary

This regulation states how the Regulations apply to dutyholders (including the self-employed).

Regulation 3(2) also provides for an exemption from the application of some of the Regulations. To benefit from the exemption, the work with asbestos must meet certain criteria.

Regulation 3

(1) These Regulations apply to a self-employed person as they apply to an employer and an employee and as if that self-employed person were both an employer and an employee.

(2) Regulations 9 (notification of work with asbestos), 18(1)(a) (designated areas) and 22 (health records and medical surveillance) do not apply where—

- *(a) the exposure to asbestos of employees is sporadic and of low intensity; and*
- *(b) it is clear from the risk assessment that the exposure to asbestos of any employee will not exceed the control limit; and*
- *(c) the work involves—*
  - *(i) short, non-continuous maintenance activities in which only non-friable materials are handled, or*
  - *(ii) removal without deterioration of non-degraded materials in which the asbestos fibres are firmly linked in a matrix, or*
  - *(iii) encapsulation or sealing of asbestos-containing materials which are in good condition, or*
  - *(iv) air monitoring and control, and the collection and analysis of samples to ascertain whether a specific material contains asbestos.*

(3) Where a duty is placed by these Regulations on an employer in respect of employees of that employer, the employer is, so far as is reasonably practicable, under a like duty in respect of any other person, whether at work or not, who may be affected by the work activity carried out by that employer except that the duties of the employer—

- *(a) under regulation 10 (information, instruction and training) do not extend to persons who are not employees of that employer unless those persons are on the premises where the work is being carried out; and*
- *(b) under regulation 22 (health records and medical surveillance) do not extend to persons who are not employees of that employer.*

(4) Regulation 17 (cleanliness of premises and plant), to the extent that it requires an employer to ensure that premises are thoroughly cleaned, does not apply—

- *(a) in England and Wales, to a fire and rescue authority within the meaning of section 1 of the Fire and Rescue Services Act 2004 or, in Scotland, the Scottish Fire and Rescue Service,[1] in respect of premises attended*

Regulation 3

by its employees for the purpose of fighting a fire or in an emergency; or

(b) to the employer of persons who attend a ship in dock premises for the purpose of fighting a fire or in an emergency, in respect of any ship so attended,

and for the purposes of this paragraph "ship" includes all vessels and hovercraft which operate on water or land and water, and "dock premises" means a dock, wharf, quay, jetty or other place at which ships load or unload goods or embark or disembark passengers, together with neighbouring land or water which is used or occupied, or intended to be used or occupied, for those or incidental activities, and any part of a ship when used for those or incidental activities.

(5) These Regulations shall not apply to the master or crew of a ship or to the employer of such persons in respect of the normal shipboard activities of a ship's crew which are carried out solely by the crew under the direction of the master, and for the purposes of this paragraph "ship" includes every description of vessel used in navigation, other than a ship forming part of Her Majesty's Navy.

1 Words substituted by the Police and Fire Reform (Scotland) Act 2012 (Consequential Modifications and Savings) Order 2013/119 (Scottish SI) Sch. 2 para 27 (April 1, 2013)

Guidance 3

Exemption from regulations 9, 18(1)(a) and 22: An overview

41 Work with asbestos includes work involving the removal, repair or disturbance of asbestos or ACMs, as well as any ancillary work and any supervision of such work.

42 All employers working with asbestos should comply with the requirements of the Regulations which help prevent and control exposure to asbestos, including:

- carrying out a risk assessment;
- planning the work;
- providing appropriate information, instruction and training to workers;
- taking measures to prevent exposure and prevent the spread of asbestos.

43 However, regulation 3(2) exempts certain types of work with asbestos from the requirements of:

- regulation 9, on notifying work with asbestos;
- regulation 18(1)(a) on designating and segregating areas where work is being carried out;
- regulation 22, on requirements for medical surveillance and keeping health records.

44 Whether the exemption applies will be decided by identifying the type of work being done and the condition and type of ACM involved, and comparing this with the exemption conditions set out in regulation 3(2)(a), (b) and (c). This should be considered as part of the risk assessment which is required before work starts (under regulation 6).

45 The exemption will not apply to:

- licensable work with asbestos;
- certain types of non-licensable work with asbestos (known as notifiable non-licensed work or NNLW).

Guidance 3

46 Licensable work does not meet the exemption conditions set out in regulations 3(2)(a) and 3(2)(b) because exposure to asbestos will not be sporadic and of low intensity and/or the risk assessment cannot clearly demonstrate that exposure will be below the control limit. As a result, the requirements of regulation 9, regulation 18(1)(a) and regulation 22 apply to all licensable work.

47 See paragraph 30–35 and Table 1 for further information on identifying if work is licensable or not.

48 See paragraph 52 for further information on whether non-licensable work meets the requirements of the exemption, or if it is NNLW.

Deciding if non-licensable work is exempt from regulations 9, 18(1)(a) and 22

49 Although it does not require a licence issued by HSE, all non-licensable work with asbestos will still need to be carried out in accordance with the requirements contained in the Regulations. In particular, it needs to be carried out by trained and competent workers in accordance with a plan of work, using appropriate control measures to prevent exposure and the spread of asbestos.

50 To decide if the exemption from the requirements in regulations 9, 18(1)(a) and 22 applies to non-licensable work, the employer needs to make an assessment of the work to be done and decide if it meets the following conditions (taken from regulation 3(2)):

- Condition 1 – the exposure to asbestos of employees is sporadic and of low intensity; and
- Condition 2 – it is clear from the risk assessment that the exposure to asbestos of any employee will not exceed the control limit; and
- Condition 3 – the work falls into one of the following categories:
  - short, non-continuous maintenance activities in which only non-friable materials are handled;
  - removal without deterioration of non-degraded materials in which the asbestos fibres are firmly linked in a matrix;
  - encapsulation or sealing of ACMs in good condition;
  - air monitoring and control, and collecting and analysing samples to establish whether a specific material contains asbestos.

51 Non-licensable work should automatically meet both Conditions 1 and 2 in paragraph 50 (otherwise it would be licensable work – see paragraph 46). In addition, for the exemption to apply, the non-licensable work should fall into one of the categories listed under Condition 3 in paragraph 50.

52 If the work has been identified as non-licensable work, because it meets Conditions 1 and 2, but does not fall within one of the categories listed under Condition 3 then it does not qualify for an exemption and is NNLW. The employer will need to follow the requirements of regulations 9, 18(1)(a) and 22. This means that, in addition to the other requirements for non-licensable work, the employer will need to:

- notify the work with asbestos to the relevant enforcing authority;
- designate the area where work with asbestos is being done;
- ensure medical examinations are carried out for workers doing NNLW;
- maintain health records for employees doing NNLW.

53 There is further information on how to notify in paragraphs 213–224.

Guidance 3

54 There is further information on the duties relating to designated areas in paragraphs 469–478.

55 There is further information on the duties relating to medical examinations for workers in paragraphs 499–507.

56 There are further examples of non-licensable work in *Asbestos essentials*.[5]

57 A decision flow chart can be found online at www.hse.gov.uk/pubns/guidance/a0.pdf.

Examples of non-licensable work and NNLW

58 It is not possible to provide definitive lists of non-licensable work and NNLW as this will depend on the circumstances of the individual work activity. However, Tables 2 and 3 provide some examples of the typical kinds of work that will and will not normally be considered to be NNLW. These tables are not intended to be exhaustive and an assessment of the potential for asbestos fibre release will be needed in cases of doubt.

59 Note that where a number of activities are being carried out on ACMs as part of a larger work activity (eg refurbishment of part of a building), the work activities should be considered collectively rather than individually when deciding if they are NNLW or not.

Table 2 Examples of non-licensable work that will not normally be NNLW

The following work activities will not normally be NNLW:
Removal of asbestos cement products, (eg roof sheeting and rainwater goods) provided the material is carefully handled/removed without breaking up; this includes work with asbestos cement which is weathered but not otherwise substantially damaged.
Maintenance work involving asbestos cement products (eg on roof sheeting and rainwater goods).
Removal of small areas of textured decorative coatings using gel/steam, to support other activities such as installation/replacement of smoke alarms and light fittings.
Removal without deterioration, of textured decorative coatings (eg if the backing board is carefully cut around to achieve virtually intact removal).
Drilling of textured decorative coatings for installation of fixtures/fittings.
Encapsulation and sealing-in work on ACMs that are in good condition (eg repairing damaged sealing material).
Removal and reattachment of loosely fixed (eg screwed) AIB panels in order to gain access to areas for other maintenance activities (eg under a bath to carry out pipework maintenance, or for access to a ceiling void for repair of lighting).
Painting/repainting AIB.

Guidance 3

Table 2 Examples of non-licensable work that will not normally be NNLW *continued*

Short duration work to repair minor damage to AIB.
Short duration work involving drilling holes in AIB (eg when installing shelving).
Maintenance work involving asbestos in ropes, yarns and woven cloth.
Maintenance work on asbestos gaskets (including removal as part of repair and upkeep of equipment).
Maintenance work involving asbestos-containing thermoplastic and vinyl floor tiles, bitumen roof felt, shingles, damp-proofing coatings, mastics.
Maintenance of asbestos-containing felt and paper.
Maintenance work involving plastic paint coatings, PVC floors, panels and sealing compounds.
Maintenance of asbestos-containing conveyor belts/drive belts, bonded rubber, electric cable.
Maintenance of resin-based ACMs such as friction products (eg brake linings).
Air and bulk sampling for asbestos fibre.

Table 3 Examples of non-licensable work that will normally be NNLW

The following work activities will normally be NNLW:
Removal of asbestos cement products (eg roof sheeting) which are substantially damaged or broken up (eg as a result of fire or flood).
Removal of asbestos cement products (eg roof sheeting) where the material will be substantially broken up, creating significant quantities of dust and debris (eg 'dropping' an asbestos cement roof).
Large-scale removal of textured decorative coatings using steaming or gelling methods (eg beyond that required for maintenance activities such as installation/replacement of smoke alarms and light fittings).
Short duration (< 2 hours) work to remove AIB as part of demolition or major refurbishment.
Short duration (< 2 hours) work on asbestos insulation.

60 To decide if work which is not listed in Tables 2 and 3 is NNLW or not, an assessment will be needed using the criteria set out in regulation 3(2). Paragraphs 58–73 provide further information.

Guidance 3

Short, non-continuous maintenance work with non-friable materials

Type of maintenance work

61 To meet the requirements of the exemption in regulation 3(2) maintenance work needs to be short and non-continuous; both of these elements will be determined by the nature of the work. Take a common sense approach to decide whether work can be short non-continuous work. For example, this type of work could include small routine building maintenance tasks, or a series of similar small tasks, or work that is carried out as part of a larger maintenance activity. Most routine work in buildings will be maintenance, such as replacing an AIB fire door or removing/replacing ceiling tiles when rewiring light fittings etc.

62 Work carried out as part of a much larger project of demolition or a total refurbishment of a building would be likely to mean it is removal rather than maintenance work.

Friable and non-friable materials

63 ACMs vary in how easily they are broken up and how readily they release asbestos fibres into the air. The more friable a material is, the more likely it will release fibres when worked on and the greater the risk of exposure.

64 Certain ACMs such as sprayed coatings on steelwork have a high tendency to release asbestos fibres and are more friable in their nature. Other ACMs have an ability to retain most fibres and are non-friable, eg if they are bound into a bonding material or matrix such as cement, bitumen, resins, rubber etc.

Removal without deterioration of non-degraded asbestos materials firmly held in a matrix

Non-degraded material

65 Non-degraded material means materials which are in good condition and capable of retaining most of the asbestos fibres. Materials that have been significantly damaged, such as by water, heat, fire or explosion, or have been crushed will be more likely to release fibres and should be considered to be degraded and therefore NNLW.

Removing ACM without deterioration

66 Whether an ACM can be removed without it breaking up (deteriorating) will need to be assessed on a case-by-case basis. If there is a reasonable expectation from the risk assessment before work starts that, given its condition on site, handling the ACM would not cause significant breakage/deterioration then the work will fall within the exemption in regulation 3(2) and will not be NNLW.

67 Deterioration includes substantial deformation. If there was minimal breakage during the work, this condition could still be met provided that most of the ACM remains virtually intact.

68 If the ACM is deliberately and substantially deteriorated when worked on or the material's matrix is significantly destroyed, the work will usually be considered to be NNLW. For example, removing substantial areas of textured decorative coatings by steaming or gelling means it will not be possible to do the work without deforming or deteriorating the coatings.

69 The condition of ACM and predicting how it will react when worked with will need to be assessed. For example, removing whole sheets of asbestos cement

Guidance 3

which are weathered, but not otherwise substantially damaged will fall within the exemption and will not be NNLW. However, if the work is carried out in such a way that will substantially break up those same sheets (eg by remote mechanical demolition), the exemption will not apply and the work will be NNLW. Also if the sheets are in such poor condition that it is not possible to remove them without significant break-up/disintegration of the cement matrix, the work is likely to be NNLW.

Asbestos fibres firmly linked in a matrix

70 Where asbestos fibres are firmly linked in a matrix, they do not normally break down easily and do not tend to release significant levels of fibres. These types of materials will only usually release fibres if work is carried out to damage the matrix, such as cutting asbestos cement sheets.

71 In certain types of ACM, the asbestos fibres will usually be firmly linked in a matrix and will not be released easily. This includes:

- asbestos cement, (unless it is substantially fragmented, crushed, or otherwise significantly damaged);
- textured decorative coatings;
- paints with asbestos, any article of bitumen, plastic, resin or rubber which contains asbestos where its thermal or acoustic properties are incidental to its main purpose, such as vinyl floor tiles, electric cables and roofing felt.

72 Work with these materials will generally not be NNLW, provided they are in good condition and the work to be done on them will not result in significant break-up or deterioration of the material.

73 There may be other materials which can be classified as firmly linked in a matrix, depending on their condition and make up, such as paper linings, cardboards, felt, textiles, gaskets, washers, and rope.

Encapsulation or sealing of ACMs in good condition

74 Work which involves the encapsulation with sealants or enclosure of ACMs, and where the condition of the materials will not lead to substantial fibre release, meets the conditions of the exemption in regulation 3(2) and will not be NNLW.

Air monitoring and control and collecting samples

75 Work involving the collection and analysis of samples to determine the presence of asbestos meets the conditions of the exemption in regulation 3(2) and will not be NNLW. The same is true for activities involving air monitoring to determine the presence of asbestos. However, these activities should be carried out in such a way that disturbance to ACMs is minimal.

ACOP 3

Employers' duties to others

76 Employers must take into account people other than their own employees in the risk assessment required by regulation 6 and in the action taken to prevent or control exposure required by regulation 11.

77 Whenever two or more employers work with asbestos or are likely to come into contact with asbestos at the same time, at the same workplace, they should co-operate to meet their separate responsibilities towards their own and each other's employees as well as other people who may be affected by the work. They should also consult relevant safety representatives and employee representatives.

Guidance 3

Table 4 Summary of employers' (and self-employed people's) duties under the Control of Asbestos Regulations 2012 in respect of employees and others

Duty of employer relating to:		*Duty for the protection of:*	
	Employees	*Other people on the premises*	*Other people likely to be affected by the work*
Regulations 5–9, 11, 13–15, 17–19 and 23	Yes	So far as is reasonably practicable	So far as is reasonably practicable
Regulation 10 – provision of information, instruction and training	Yes	So far as is reasonably practicable	No
Regulation 22 – health records and medical surveillance	Yes	No	No

78 As set out in Table 4, some employers' duties to other people, not employed by them, extend so far as is reasonable practicable. Further explanation of the term 'reasonably practicable' is provided on HSE's website at www.hse.gov.uk/risk/faq.htm. In relation to the Regulations this will generally focus on ensuring that those who may be affected by work on asbestos are:

- prevented from entering contaminated areas;
- not exposed to asbestos as a result of the work being done;
- provided with enough information to avoid risks from the work area.

79 In particular, the risk assessment (regulation 6) and plan of work (regulation 7) and the control measures used should take account of people not directly employed by the employer but who could be affected by work being done on asbestos. This includes contractors and other employees working on the premises for other employers; other people occupying the premises; members of the public and other visitors etc.

Duties under other regulations

80 There are other people associated with the work covered by this ACOP who may not have direct duties under the Regulations but may well have duties under other legislation. This may include analysts, coordinators, clients, designers and principal contractors as defined by the Construction (Design and Management) Regulations 2007 (CDM).[6] People carrying out site clearance certification (eg analysts) may have general duties under sections 2, 3, 7, 8, 36 or 37 of the HSW Act.

Regulation 4 Duty to manage asbestos in non-domestic premises

Summary

This regulation covers the duty to manage asbestos in non-domestic premises. It requires dutyholders to identify the location and condition of asbestos in non-domestic premises and to manage the risk to prevent harm to anyone who works on the building or to building occupants. It also explains what is required of people who have a duty to co-operate with the main dutyholder to enable them to comply with the regulation. Non-domestic premises includes the common parts of domestic premises.

Regulation 4

(1) In this regulation "the dutyholder" means—

(a) every person who has, by virtue of a contract or tenancy, an obligation of any extent in relation to the maintenance or repair of non-domestic premises or any means of access or egress to or from those premises; or
(b) in relation to any part of non-domestic premises where there is no such contract or tenancy, every person who has, to any extent, control of that part of those non-domestic premises or any means of access or egress to or from those premises.

and where there is more than one such dutyholder, the relative contribution to be made by each such person in complying with the requirements of this regulation will be determined by the nature and extent of the maintenance and repair obligation owed by that person.

(2) Every person must cooperate with the dutyholder so far as is necessary to enable the dutyholder to comply with the duties set out under this regulation.

(3) In order to manage the risk from asbestos in non-domestic premises, the dutyholder must ensure that a suitable and sufficient assessment is carried out as to whether asbestos is or is liable to be present in the premises.

(4) In making the assessment—

(a) such steps as are reasonable in the circumstances must be taken; and
(b) the condition of any asbestos which is, or has been assumed to be, present in the premises must be considered.

(5) Without prejudice to the generality of paragraph (4), the dutyholder must ensure that—

(a) account is taken of building plans or other relevant information and of the age of the premises; and
(b) an inspection is made of those parts of the premises which are reasonably accessible.

(6) The dutyholder must ensure that the assessment is reviewed without delay if—

(a) there is reason to suspect that the assessment is no longer valid; or
(b) there has been a significant change in the premises to which the assessment relates.

Regulation 4

(7) The dutyholder must ensure that the conclusions of the assessment and every review are recorded.

(8) Where the assessment shows that asbestos is or is liable to be present in any part of the premises the dutyholder must ensure that—

(a) a determination of the risk from that asbestos is made;
(b) a written plan identifying those parts of the premises concerned is prepared; and
(c) the measures which are to be taken for managing the risk are specified in the written plan.

(9) The measures to be specified in the plan for managing the risk must include adequate measures for—

(a) monitoring the condition of any asbestos or any substance containing or suspected of containing asbestos;
(b) ensuring any asbestos or any such substance is properly maintained or where necessary safely removed; and
(c) ensuring that information about the location and condition of any asbestos or any such substance is—
(i) provided to every person liable to disturb it, and
(ii) made available to the emergency services.

(10) The dutyholder must ensure that—

(a) the plan is reviewed and revised at regular intervals, and without delay if—
(i) there is reason to suspect that the plan is no longer valid, or
(ii) there has been a significant change in the premises to which the plan relates;
(b) the measures specified in the plan are implemented; and
(c) the measures taken to implement the plan are recorded.

(11) In this regulation—

(a) "the assessment" is a reference to the assessment required by paragraph (3);
(b) "the plan" is a reference to the plan required by paragraph (8); and
(c) "the premises" is a reference to the non-domestic premises referred to in paragraph (1).

ACOP 4

Managing the risk

81 The dutyholder must manage the risk from asbestos on the premises.

82 The main dutyholder is required to ensure that a written plan is prepared that shows where the ACM is located and how it will be managed to prevent exposure to asbestos, including to contractors and other workers who may carry out work on the fabric of the building that could disturb the ACM. This plan then needs to be put into action and communicated to those affected. The dutyholder needs to ensure the plan is reviewed regularly and updated as circumstances change, in consultation with all those who may be affected.

Guidance 4

83 The regulation is designed to make sure anyone who carries out any work in non-domestic premises and any occupants of the premises are not exposed to asbestos from ACMs that may be present.

Guidance 4

84 The regulation identifies those who have the main responsibilities (ie dutyholders) under the regulation and places certain duties on them. Dutyholders must ensure risks from the presence of asbestos in the premises are managed. The regulation also requires additional groups to co-operate with, or provide information to, the main dutyholder.

85 In practice, the duty to manage requires the main dutyholder to make sure that competent persons:

- assess whether the premises are liable to contain asbestos and identify its location and condition (or, alternatively, assume asbestos is present and manage the premises accordingly);
- assess the risk from any located (or assumed) ACMs and to identify vulnerable or damaged ACMs and arrange for their repair and/or protection or, where necessary, arrange removal by somebody competent to do this.

86 An essential part of the duty to manage is making sure that information on the location and condition of the ACM is passed on to contractors and other workers who may carry out work on the fabric of the building that could damage/disturb asbestos. This allows them to put in place appropriate controls to protect themselves and others in the building.

87 To help the main dutyholder and others who have duties under this regulation, paragraphs 88–147 give guidance on:

- where the duty to manage applies;
- where the duty to manage applies to common parts of domestic premises;
- identifying who the dutyholders are;
- who has a duty to co-operate with the dutyholder;
- what the dutyholder must do to comply with the law.

Where the duty to manage applies

88 The duty to manage covers all non-domestic premises. This includes all industrial and commercial buildings, such as factories, warehouses, offices and shops. The duty also covers public buildings such as hospitals, schools, museums, libraries, leisure centres, churches and other religious buildings. In addition, premises include road and rail vehicles, vessels, aircraft and offshore installations, as well as structures and installations (such as bridges), street furniture (such as street lighting) etc.

89 The duty does not apply to domestic premises such as private houses. However, the duty does apply to the 'common parts' of multi–occupancy domestic premises, such as purpose-built flats or houses converted into flats. The common parts of such domestic premises might include foyers, corridors, lifts and lift shafts, staircases, roof spaces, gardens, yards, outhouses and garages but not the private domestic area inside each flat.

90 Common parts do not include rooms within a private residence that are shared by more than one household such as bathrooms and kitchens in shared houses and communal dining rooms and lounges in sheltered accommodation.

Common parts of domestic premises

91 Table 5 sets out examples of if and where the duty to manage is likely to apply to parts of domestic premises.

92 Note that even where the duty to manage under regulation 4 does not apply, Section 3 of the HSW Act does apply to anyone conducting a business, such as

Guidance 4

landlords of domestic premises. The section 3 duty stipulates that an employer or self-employed person must ensure so far as is reasonably practicable that the conduct of their undertaking does not present a risk to the health and safety of people who are not their employees.

Table 5 Duty to manage in common parts of domestic premises

Type of residence	Type of occupation	Rooms or parts	Duty to manage applies?
Private house – single dwelling including bedsits	Owner occupier	All	No
	Let to single family	All	No
	Occupied by more than one family	Private rooms, eg bedroom, living room	No
		Shared rooms, eg kitchen, bathroom, lavatory	No
	Rooms let to lodgers	Common parts for access and circulation, eg entrance hall, staircase	No
		Private rooms	No
House converted into flats	Occupied by more than one family	Private rooms	No
		Common parts for access, circulation and storage, eg entrance hall, staircase, roof space	Yes
Garages, parking spaces	Integral to, or linked with residence	Private	No
	Not allocated to any specific person	Common parts – for access and circulation	Yes
Block of flats	Occupied by more than one family	Individual flats	No
		Common parts, eg foyer, lift, stairs, lobby, boiler and plant room, roof space, communal yard, garden, store rooms, bike shelter, external outbuilding	Yes

Guidance 4

Table 5 Duty to manage in common parts of domestic premises *(continued)*

Type of residence	Type of occupation	Rooms or parts	Duty to manage applies?
Flats over a shop or office, with or without a separate entrance	Occupied by the shop or office owner	Private rooms	No
	Leased separately	Private rooms	No
		Access and circulation areas	Yes
Sheltered accommodation		Private rooms	No
		Common rooms, eg dining room, lounge	No
		Work areas, eg kitchen, staff room, laundry	Yes
		Common parts, eg foyer, lift, stairs, circulation areas, boiler room, store rooms, roof space, external outbuilding	Yes
Hotel, pubs, guest house, hall of residence, hostel (private and local authority), care home	Includes bed and breakfast, if that is the main purpose	Private rooms occupied by the owner	No
		Guest accommodation and common parts (eg foyer, lift, stairs, circulation areas), store rooms, roof space, outbuildings	Yes
Tied cottage/ accommodation	Leased or rent-free	All	No
Farm	Leased or rent-free	Farmhouse	No
		Farm buildings	Yes

ACOP 4

Identifying dutyholders

93 The duty to manage is placed on the person or organisation that has the main responsibility for maintenance or repair of non-domestic premises and common parts of domestic premises. The dutyholder may be the owner or, where there is an explicit agreement, such as a tenancy agreement or contract, the dutyholder may be the occupier or the landlord, sub-lessor or managing agent. It may also be the tenant. Where there is a tenancy agreement or contract, the extent of the duty will depend on the nature of that agreement. In some circumstances, the duty to manage may be shared. If so, the dutyholders should co-operate to make sure that the risk from asbestos is managed appropriately.

94 The extent of the duty will, in most cases, be determined by the degree of responsibility over matters concerning the fabric of the building and the maintenance activities carried out there. For example, the owner may rent out or lease workplace premises under agreements where the tenants are responsible for all alterations, maintenance and repairs in the premises. In such situations, the tenants will be the dutyholder.

95 There may be no tenancy agreement or contract or, if there is, it may not specify who has responsibility for the maintenance or repair of non-domestic premises. In these cases, or where the premises are unoccupied, the duty is placed on whoever has ultimate control of the premises, or part of the premises, eg the owner.

Guidance 4

Dutyholders for public buildings

96 The identity of the dutyholder in public buildings, such as hospitals, schools and similar premises will depend on how responsibility for maintenance of the premises is allocated. For example in most schools, the dutyholder will be the employer. Who the employer is varies with the type of school. For local authority managed schools, eg community schools and voluntary-controlled schools, the employer is the local authority. For voluntary-aided and foundation schools, it will be the school governors, and for academy and Free Schools, the academy trust will be the employer.
For independent and fee-paying schools, it may be the proprietor, governors or trustees. Budgets for repair and maintenance of school buildings are sometimes delegated to schools by a local authority, with capital expenditure remaining the responsibility of the local authority. In such cases, the duty to manage asbestos is shared between schools and the local authority.

ACOP 4

Deciding who has the duty to manage

97 In situations where there is no owner with sole responsibility for maintenance of the premises, it will be necessary to consult the detail of any contract/tenancy agreement to help establish who is responsible for which aspects of the requirements, under regulation 4.

ACOP 4

98 Table 6 shows some examples of tenancy arrangements and how responsibilities may be allocated or shared under the regulation.

Table 6 Identity of dutyholders

Responsibility for premises	**Who has the duty to manage under regulation 4?**
The owner has sole responsibility for the premises or has sole responsibility for the common parts of multi-occupied buildings	The owner
Under a tenancy agreement or contract, tenants (including employers or occupiers) are responsible for alterations, repairs and maintenance	The tenant, or tenants, in multi-occupancy premises
Under a tenancy agreement or contract, the owner keeps responsibility for maintenance and repairs, and the owner has control of access by maintenance workers into the building	The owner
Under a tenancy agreement or contract, responsibility is shared between several people, eg owners, sub-lessors, occupiers and employers	Each party – for those parts of the premises for which they have maintenance responsibilities Note that employers occupying the premises also have a general duty of co-operation to comply with the requirement of any health and safety regulations under regulation 11 of the Management of Health and Safety at Work Regulations 1999[7]
If an owner/leaseholder uses a managing agent	The owner The managing agent would act on behalf of the owner but does not assume the owner's duties in law. The ultimate responsibility remains with the owner
There is no tenancy agreement or contract	The person in control of the premises
The premises are unoccupied	The person in control of the premises

Changes in tenancy or occupation

99 If the terms of the tenancy are altered or if the building is vacated, the owner or leaseholder must make sure all relevant information is passed on to any new occupier.

ACOP 4

Duty to co-operate

100 If the owner rents, leases or lets out under a contract or agreement and gives shared responsibility to the owner and the occupier(s), all parties should make whatever parts of the building they are responsible for available to one another. This enables each dutyholder to carry out their responsibilities under regulation 4.

101 Anyone who is not a dutyholder, but has information on or control of the premises, must help the dutyholder, as far as necessary, to comply with the duty. But this does not extend to paying for or sharing the costs of any actions the dutyholder takes to manage these risks.

Guidance 4

102 Some examples of where the duty to co-operate applies are listed below.

- An owner who has no maintenance and repair responsibilities for the premises would still need to provide any information they have on the building to help to confirm if there are ACMs present or not.
- Architects, surveyors or building contractors who were involved in the construction or maintenance of the building are expected to make this information available at a justifiable and reasonable cost.
- Those in occupation of the premises, who have no maintenance or repair responsibilities, but may still control access to the premises, are required to co-operate by allowing the dutyholder access to carry out the actions needed to comply with the duty.
- Where the duty to manage is shared between two or more dutyholders, they must co-operate to make sure they comply with the requirements of regulation 4.
- In public buildings, such as hospitals and schools where the employees of a number of employers must work together, to allow the dutyholder to comply with the requirements of the Regulations.

ACOP 4

Delegating tasks

103 The dutyholder's legal responsibilities cannot be delegated, but dutyholders can nominate others to do all or part of the work to assist in complying with the duties. Anyone or any organisation who is nominated to do some work as a result of this regulation must know what it is they have to do and be able to do it safely. They should be competent to do this work.

104 Safety representatives must be consulted about the arrangements to appoint a competent person or organisation.

Guidance 4

105 The dutyholder must satisfy themselves that any person or organisation nominated to assist them in complying with the duty to manage:

- can demonstrate suitable competence and training;
- can demonstrate independence, impartiality and integrity;
- has an adequate management system in place;
- carries out any survey commissioned to locate ACMs, in accordance with recommended guidance.

106 Where the dutyholder appoints a third party to carry out a survey, they can assess if the surveyor is likely to have adequate experience and training by checking that they are accredited by a recognised accreditation body as complying with BS EN ISO/IEC 17020[8] to undertake surveys for ACMs. UKAS is currently the sole recognised accreditation body in Great Britain.

Guidance 4

107 If the dutyholder selects a surveyor who is not accredited by UKAS, they should make reasonable enquiries to make sure that they are competent by obtaining details of their qualifications, copies of their written procedures (including quality control policies) and references to other evidence of recent similar work.

108 HSE strongly recommends using accredited surveyors.

109 In accordance with the Safety Representatives and Safety Committees Regulations 1977, safety representatives should be consulted on matters affecting the employees they represent. This means they should be consulted about the arrangements and, with reasonable notice being given, see any records made in connection with the assessment.

110 Similarly, employees not represented by trade union representatives should be consulted in accordance with The Health and Safety (Consultation with Employees) Regulations 1996.

ACOP 4

111 Where the dutyholder has nominated a person or organisation to assist in complying their responsibilities, they must make sure that those on the premises are aware who has been nominated and the tasks they have been given.

What the dutyholders must do to comply with the law

112 Dutyholders are required to ensure that:

- **reasonable steps are taken to find materials in premises likely to contain asbestos and to check their condition;**
- **materials are presumed to contain asbestos unless there is strong evidence that they do not;**
- **a written record of the location and condition of asbestos and/or presumed ACMs is made and that the record is kept up to date;**
- **the risk of anyone being exposed to these materials is assessed;**
- **a written plan to manage that risk is prepared and that the plan is put into effect to make sure that:**
  - **any material known or presumed to contain asbestos is kept in a good state of repair;**
  - **any material that contains or is presumed to contain asbestos is, because of the risks associated with its location or condition, repaired and adequately protected or, if it is in a vulnerable position and cannot be adequately repaired or protected, it is removed;**
  - **information on the location and condition of the material is given to anyone who is liable to disturb it or is otherwise potentially at risk.**

Find out if asbestos is present

113 Everything that can reasonably be done must be done to decide whether there is (or may be) asbestos in the premises, and if there is asbestos (or could be), to find out where it is likely to be. All documentary information that can be obtained about the premises must be systematically checked and as thorough an inspection, as is reasonably accessible, of the premises both inside and outside must be carried out.

114 The thorough inspection of the premises will usually take the form of a survey. The survey should be comprehensive and systematic and the survey type should ensure that the dutyholder meets their current occupational requirements: a management survey should be carried out to identify the

ACOP 4

asbestos for normal day-to-day occupation and maintenance of the building, and a refurbishment and demolition survey should refurbishment or demolition work be planned.

115 All parts of the premises should be checked, including warehouses, yards, sheds, outbuildings, underfloor services, ducts, corridors, vertical risers, ceiling voids, storerooms, external runs of pipes and bridges. Fixed plant and machinery, such as process plant, should be included, as well as mobile units which are permanently on the premises. Mobile units, which are only on the premises intermittently, should not be included.

116 The dutyholder should ensure that anyone who may be able to provide more information (and in any case have a duty of co-operation) is consulted and that this information is obtained. Such people may include:

- **architects;**
- **building surveyors;**
- **building contractors;**
- **safety representatives;**
- **employees who are familiar with the premises;**
- **the previous dutyholder.**

117 There may also be previous assessments and surveys or other existing documents which can be consulted. Check any information obtained or provided for accuracy.

118 Consider the age of the premises when assessing if asbestos is present. Any premises whose construction was completed before 2000 should always be presumed to contain asbestos, unless there is strong evidence to suggest they do not. Any premises constructed after 2000 can be presumed to be asbestos free. However, exercise caution in circumstances where new premises are built on existing basements or linked to adjoining structures.

119 If the building's age or the information provides very strong evidence that no ACMs are present, no further action is needed other than to record why this evidence indicates there is no asbestos present.

Assessing the condition of ACMs

120 The condition of ACMs should be assessed. The assessment should take account of the type of ACM, the amount and its condition. This will determine its potential to release asbestos fibres into the air, if disturbed. The assessment should consider the following:

- **Is the surface of the material damaged, frayed or scratched?**
- **Are the surface sealants peeling or breaking off?**
- **Is the material becoming detached from its base? (This is a particular problem with pipe and boiler lagging and sprayed coatings.)**
- **Are protective coverings, designed to protect the material, missing or damaged?**
- **Is there asbestos dust or debris from damage near the material?**

Guidance 4

Assessing the risk

121 The dutyholder should ensure that an assessment of the potential risk from the ACMs is made. The assessment should consider the following:

- The information gathered on the location, amount and condition of the ACM.
- Is the ACM in a position where it is likely to be disturbed?
- How much ACM is present?

Guidance 4

- Is there easy access to the ACM?
- Do people work or move near the ACM in a way that is liable to disturb it, ie is it vulnerable to damage?
- If likely to be disturbed, is it close to areas where people normally work?
- How many people use the area where the ACM is?
- Is maintenance, repair or refurbishment work or other activity on the premises likely to be carried out where the ACM is?

122 The assessment should identify how the ACMs are going to be managed and how any work activity which may disturb asbestos will be managed. The assessment should identify those ACMs:

- which are in good condition and can be left in place and managed;
- which are in vulnerable locations that need to be protected or removed;
- in poor condition and which need repair or removal;
- which will need to be removed where maintenance, refurbishment work or demolition is planned.

Recording the assessment information

123 Create a record of the locations where the assessment indicates ACMs are present or presumed to be present. The written record should include an accurate drawing of the premises and the main features of each room and passageways should be marked on it.

124 The record and drawing should contain details of the locations of the ACMs, their extent and condition and their forms (eg the product type – tiles, boards, cement sheets) and what the ACM looks like (eg if painted and what colour).

125 The record and drawings should record details of any area not accessed or inspected and the area must be assumed to contain asbestos unless there is strong evidence that it does not.

126 This formal record is frequently referred to as an asbestos register. It can be in written or electronic form.

127 The record should be dated to aid periodic reviews.

128 All the information gathered from the assessment should be used to form the management plan.

ACOP 4

Making the management plan

129 A written (electronic or paper) management plan should be prepared. The management plan should set out how the risks identified from asbestos will be managed. Details should include:

- **identifying the person(s) responsible for managing the asbestos risk;**
- **a copy of the asbestos record or register and how to access it if it is kept electronically;**
- **instructions that any work on the fabric of the building cannot start without the relevant parts of the record/register being checked. The plan should include details for how this will be achieved. In particular, the plan should identify the procedures and arrangements to make sure:**
  - **the record/register is checked in good time before the work starts;**
  - **checks will be made that the information on the presence of asbestos has been understood and will be taken into account;**
  - **checks will be made that the correct controls will be used and that competent asbestos-trained contractors will carry out the work;**

ACOP 4

- plans for any necessary work identified from the risk assessment, eg repair, protect or remove ACMs;
- the schedule for monitoring the condition of any ACMs;
- how to communicate the content of the management plan;
- contingency arrangements if the main contact person for asbestos risk management is not available.

Actioning the management plan

130 The dutyholder should ensure that the plan is implemented to manage the risks. The action plan should:

- prioritise the actions identified;
- give high priority to damaged material and materials likely to be disturbed; these will need to be repaired, sealed, enclosed protectively or removed using trained and competent personnel.

131 If unsure how to implement the management plan themselves, the dutyholder should seek competent specialist advice from an asbestos surveyor, a laboratory or a licensed contractor, or other competent person as appropriate.

132 The plan should include procedures and responsibilities to ensure that the asbestos register is shared with any worker/contractor carrying out maintenance or other work.

133 The asbestos register, including drawings, should be available on site for the entire life of the premises and should be kept up to date.

134 Work should only start once the dutyholder is satisfied that the information in the asbestos record/register is known and understood by the workers who are doing the work on site and easily accessible for anyone who needs to inspect it.

Guidance 4

Managing asbestos left in place

135 If the material is in good condition, well protected either by its position or physical protection, reducing the likelihood of damage, and is unlikely to be worked on regularly or otherwise disturbed, it is usually safer to leave it in place and manage it.

Leaving asbestos in place

136 If ACMs or presumed ACMs that are in good condition are left in place, this information should be entered on the record/register of locations and the information kept up to date.

137 Everyone who needs to know about the asbestos should be told about its presence in sufficient detail, eg maintenance workers, contractors and occupants. People who simply occupy premises only need to be informed, where necessary, of the location of the ACMs, so that the ACM will not be disturbed during normal occupational activities. Occupants should be instructed not to do anything which could damage or disturb the ACMs and to report any accidental damage promptly.

138 ACMs can be labelled clearly with the asbestos warning sign (see Schedule 2) or some other warning system (eg colour coding) can be used. If labelling is not used, the dutyholder must make sure that those who might work on the material know that it contains or may contain asbestos, before they start work.

139 It can save time and prevent confusion if the location of non-asbestos material, which could be mistaken for asbestos, is noted in the asbestos register and drawing.

Guidance 4

Repair and removal of asbestos

140 Some damaged ACM can be made safe by repairing it and either sealing or enclosing it to prevent further damage. If this can be done safely, the dutyholder should ensure the area is marked after it has been repaired and make sure it is on the record of asbestos locations.

141 If ACM is likely to be disturbed during routine maintenance work or daily use of the building, it will release fibres. If it cannot be easily repaired and protected, the dutyholder should have it removed.

142 This work must be carried out by someone trained and competent to carry out licensable work, NNLW, or non-licensable work, as appropriate.

ACOP 4

Reviewing and updating the management plan

143 As a minimum, the management plan, including records and drawings, should be reviewed every 12 months. It should also be reviewed if there is reason to believe that circumstances have changed (eg there is a change of use of building, work being undertaken, ACMs removed or repaired etc). The plan, including records and drawings, should then be updated accordingly.

144 Any identified or suspected ACM must be inspected and its condition assessed periodically, to check that it has not deteriorated or been damaged. The frequency of inspection will depend on the location of the ACMs and other factors which could affect their condition, eg the activities in the building, non-occupancy etc. There will also be events or changes, eg maintenance work, new tenants or employees, that should also trigger a review of the plan.

Guidance 4

145 The effectiveness of the current management plan should be reviewed to:

- highlight the need for action to repair/remove ACMs;
- raise awareness among all employees;
- raise issues which may affect the management plan, including:
  - changes to the organisational structure and/or staff;
  - resourcing the management plan;
  - changes to company procedures;
  - changes in building use/occupancy/refurbishment plans;
  - any instances of failure of the procedures, eg where procedures have not been followed and why not; where procedures have been inadequate and why; and where exposure to airborne asbestos fibres has occurred.

ACOP 4

146 There should be periodic checks to make sure that the arrangements and procedures for managing asbestos are working and that people are fully aware of what they should be doing to comply with the duty to manage.

Communicating and sharing the management plan

147 Dutyholders should ensure that the management plan is made available to all the individual premises, so if there are separate site managers/building managers responsible for different premises on the same site, they must each make the information available to those in their respective premises. Dutyholders should:

- **tell employees what the management plan arrangements are;**
- **provide the emergency services with information on the location and condition of any known ACMs;**
- **provide copies of the management plan for employee representatives and trade union safety representatives.**

Regulation 5 Identification of the presence of asbestos

Summary

This regulation requires employers to identify the presence of asbestos and its type and condition before any building, maintenance, demolition or other work, liable to disturb asbestos, begins. It also sets out the requirement to arrange a survey if existing information on the presence of asbestos in the premises is incomplete or appears unreliable.

Regulation 5

(1) An employer must not undertake work in demolition, maintenance, or any other work which exposes or is liable to expose employees of that employer to asbestos in respect of any premises unless either—

(a) that employer has carried out a suitable and sufficient assessment as to whether asbestos, what type of asbestos, contained in what material and in what condition is present or is liable to be present in those premises; or

(b) if there is doubt as to whether asbestos is present in those premises that employer—

(i) assumes that asbestos is present, and that it is not chrysotile alone, and

(ii) observes the applicable provisions of these Regulations.

ACOP 5

148 Before carrying out any work involving the potential disturbance of asbestos, employers should find out if the part of the building likely to be disturbed contains asbestos and, if so, the type and condition. This should include assessing relevant information, such as that contained in construction plans or provided by dutyholders responsible for the maintenance and repair of premises under regulation 4 of the Regulations (eg asbestos surveys or registers). If no records are available, or there are doubts about their accuracy/relevance, employers may need to arrange a survey and analysis of representative samples to determine the presence, type and condition of asbestos.

149 Alternatively, employers should assume that the part of the building to be disturbed contains the most hazardous types of asbestos, crocidolite (blue) or amosite (brown), and apply the appropriate control measures required by the Regulations, using a licensed contractor if required.

Guidance 5

150 Information on the presence of asbestos can be found from a variety of sources, including records of construction and building plans, and information provided by dutyholders responsible for the maintenance and repair of premises. Dutyholders responsible for the maintenance and repair of premises have an obligation under regulation 4(9)(c) to inform anyone liable to disturb ACMs, including maintenance workers, about the presence and condition of such materials.

151 Employers will need to assess the accuracy of information in surveys and plans provided to them and also their relevance to the location and type of work to be done in the building. For example:

- has the survey been carried out by a person competent to do so?
- does the the building layout match that in the survey/plan provided?
- does information on the condition of the ACMs in the survey/plan match what is seen on site?

Guidance 5

- is the information in the survey/plan relevant to the work to be done (eg ACMs in voids behind walls, or similar hard to access positions, may not have been included in the survey/plan)?

152 For construction projects within scope of the Construction (Design and Management) Regulations, clients have to provide pre-construction information to designers and contractors. This will include information held by the client (eg in an existing health and safety file), or reasonably obtained, on the presence of asbestos and its type and condition. It is important that employers coming onto site after construction work has started co-operate with others engaged on that project over any existing construction phase plan.

Regulation 6 Assessment of work which exposes employees to asbestos

Summary

This regulation requires employers to carry out a risk assessment to identify the risks of exposure to asbestos. It sets out the requirement to record any significant findings and put in place steps to prevent, or reduce, exposure to employees.

Regulation 6

(1) An employer must not carry out work which is liable to expose employees of that employer to asbestos unless that employer has—

(a) made a suitable and sufficient assessment of the risk created by that exposure to the health of those employees and of the steps that need to be taken to meet the requirements of these Regulations;
(b) recorded the significant findings of that risk assessment as soon as is practicable after the risk assessment is made; and
(c) implemented the steps referred to in sub-paragraph (a).

(2) Without prejudice to the generality of paragraph (1), the risk assessment must—

(a) subject to regulation 5, identify the type of asbestos to which employees are liable to be exposed;
(b) determine the nature and degree of exposure which may occur in the course of the work;
(c) consider the effects of control measures which have been or will be taken in accordance with regulation 11;
(d) consider the results of monitoring of exposure in accordance with regulation 19;
(e) set out the steps to be taken to prevent that exposure or reduce it to the lowest level reasonably practicable;
(f) consider the results of any medical surveillance that is relevant; and
(g) include such additional information as the employer may need in order to complete the risk assessment.

(3) The risk assessment must be reviewed regularly, and immediately if—

(a) there is reason to suspect that the existing risk assessment is no longer valid;
(b) there is a significant change in the work to which the risk assessment relates; or
(c) the results of any monitoring carried out pursuant to regulation 19 show it to be necessary,

Regulation 6

and where, as a result of the review, changes to the risk assessment are required, those changes must be made and, where they relate to the significant findings of the risk assessment or are themselves significant, recorded.

(4) Where, in accordance with the requirement in paragraph (2)(b), the risk assessment has determined that the exposure to asbestos of employees of that employer may exceed the control limit, the employer must keep a copy of the significant findings of the risk assessment at those premises at which, and for such time as, the work to which that risk assessment relates is being carried out.

Guidance 6

General requirements for risk assessments

153 Regulation 6 should be read with regulation 11(1), which places a duty on employers to entirely prevent the exposure of their employees to asbestos so far as is reasonably practicable and this should be the first consideration. If this is not possible, the exposure must be reduced to the lowest level reasonably practicable. The risk assessment must identify how to achieve this and if there are any other risks in complying with this duty. For example if cables are rerouted to avoid disturbing ACMs, the risk assessment should consider what other risks the workers would face and what the overall risk would be. Consider general risks too, as required by regulation 3 of the Management of Health and Safety at Work Regulations 1999.

ACOP 6

154 If work liable to expose employees, and others affected by the work, to asbestos is unavoidable then, before starting work, employers must make a suitable and sufficient assessment of the risks created by the likely exposure. Employers must then identify the steps required to comply with the Regulations. Whoever carries out the risk assessment must:

- **carry it out in time to comply with the Regulations and enable appropriate precautions to be taken before work begins;**
- **make sure the assessment is job specific and considers the full scope of the work;**
- **establish the extent of potential risks and who could be affected;**
- **identify the steps taken to remove the risk or, if that is not possible, to reduce the risk;**
- **record significant findings in writing (electronic or paper);**
- **communicate significant findings to employees and anyone else who could be affected in an understandable way, as appropriate, to minimise risks to them or to take appropriate precautions to reduce/remove the risk before work begins;**
- **review the assessment regularly and update it as required.**

Guidance 6

Involving employees

155 Employers have duties under the Safety Representatives and Safety Committees Regulations 1977 and the Health and Safety (Consultation with Employees) Regulations 1996 (as amended) to consult their employees. It can be helpful for employers to involve employees during the risk assessment, to help determine the real nature and degree of their exposure. Appropriate consultation can also make a significant contribution to creating and maintaining a safe and healthy working environment and an effective health and safety culture.

ACOP 6

Competency to carry out a risk assessment

156 Employers must make sure that whoever carries out the risk assessment and provides advice on the prevention and control of exposure is competent to do this. Whoever carries out the risk assessment should:

- have adequate knowledge, training and expertise in understanding the risks from asbestos and be able to make informed and appropriate decisions about the risks and precautions needed;
- know how the work activity may disturb asbestos;
- be familiar with and understand the requirements of the Regulations;
- have the ability and authority to collate all the necessary and relevant information;
- be able to assess other non-asbestos risks on site;
- be able to estimate the expected level of exposure to decide whether or not the control limit is likely to be exceeded.

Suitable and sufficient risk assessment

157 To be suitable and sufficient, the risk assessment should include:

- for non-licensable work, a statement of why the work meets the criteria for non-licensable rather than licensable work, and whether it is NNLW;
- a description of the work being carried out and the expected scale and duration;
- a description of the type(s) of asbestos and results of any survey or analysis or a statement that the assumption is that the asbestos is not chrysotile alone;
- a description of the quantity, form, size, means of attachment, extent and condition of the ACMs present.

158 Details of expected exposures should be recorded and include:

- data on the concentration of asbestos fibres likely to be present, including the source for this information;
- whether they are liable to exceed the control limit and the number of people likely to be affected;
- the level of expected exposure, so that suitable personal protective equipment (PPE) and respiratory protective equipment (RPE) can be selected;
- whether anyone other than employees may be exposed, and their expected exposures;
- whether intermittent higher exposures may arise and their expected frequency and duration;
- any results already available from air monitoring in similar circumstances.

159 The steps to take to control exposure to the lowest level reasonably practicable should also be recorded, eg:

- the type of controlled wetting and method of application;
- using local exhaust ventilation (LEV);
- using a glovebag;
- wrap and cut;
- the use of low dust methods;
- shadow vacuuming.

ACOP 6

160 The risk assessment should also include:

- **the steps taken to control the release of asbestos into the environment, eg enclosures with negative pressure and entry and exit procedures. Where it is not considered practicable to use an enclosure, a full justification is required, and clear advice on what action to take if there is an accidental release;**
- **details of the decontamination procedures, including using hygiene units where appropriate, and for transferring and removing waste, including contaminated tools and equipment;**
- **procedures for the selection, provision, use and decontamination or disposal of PPE/RPE;**
- **procedures for dealing with emergencies;**
- **any other information relevant to safe working practices, such as other significant non-asbestos hazards like working at height or in confined spaces;**
- **management arrangements for ensuring that risks are adequately controlled during the work.**

161 The findings of the risk assessment as detailed above are all deemed to be significant and must be recorded, as required by regulation 6(1)(b), and available on site at all times.

Guidance 6

Identifying the type of ACM

162 Knowing the type of ACM (eg AIB, asbestos insulation, asbestos coating, asbestos cement, asbestos-containing textured decorative coatings) and the work method proposed is necessary to:

- estimate the potential fibre release for assessment purposes;
- select the most appropriate handling and removal techniques, or combinations of techniques;
- determine whether the work is licensable (or NNLW).

163 It is essential to be able to distinguish between asbestos cement and AIB. If in doubt, employers should assume the material is AIB and take precautions accordingly.

164 For ancillary work involving the testing and maintenance of plant and equipment, the asbestos is most likely to be in the form of dust and the type of ACM may not be relevant. The condition of the material can have a significant effect on the assessment. Knowing the extent of the material (eg its length and span, whether it extends into other rooms and work areas) is also important so that the number of enclosures required, and arrangements for the transfer/removal of waste, can be properly assessed. This will identify what work is being done and which ACMs will remain in place, and clarify the areas where there may need to be a certificate for reoccupation. See paragraphs 430–467 for information about clearance procedures and certificates for reoccupation.

ACOP 6

Additional risk assessment requirements for licensable work

165 For the risk assessment for licensable work to be suitable and sufficient it should, in addition to those elements outlined in paragraphs 157–160, record the reasons for the chosen work method and arrangements required to ensure that the premises or parts of the premises where work has taken place are left clean for reoccupation and include:

ACOP 6

- detail of the areas which need a certificate for reoccupation;
- consideration of potential problems for issuing the certificate for reoccupation and how they can be avoided or dealt with before work starts, eg earth floors, limpet spray ingrained in concrete or tar-like layers, wet areas which cannot be dried out and the presence of ACMs which will remain in the areas after the work is complete;
- consideration of the need for pre-cleaning to remove ACMs or suspected ACMs. The pre-cleaning assessment should include identifying the control measures to prevent release of asbestos fibres.

All these points are significant and must be recorded as required by regulation 6(1)(b) and available on site at all times.

Work in elevated temperatures and hot conditions

166 Work with asbestos in hot and humid conditions should be avoided as far as possible, as it creates significant additional risks for asbestos workers. Such work will only be permitted in rare and exceptional circumstances and only when all possible alternatives and control options have been considered. If the work can be justified, additional precautions, as identified in the risk assessment, must be taken to prevent heat stress and other risks. The precautions will include:

- restricting when the work is to be carried out to times with cooler ambient temperatures;
- reducing work periods;
- introducing cool air to the work area (eg air conditioning);
- having measures in place to prevent dehydration when operators have left the work area, eg providing cool drinks free of charge in the rest facility;
- using enclosures with increased sizes and ventilation rates;
- where possible, shutting down or shielding/insulating any hot plant and equipment to be worked on or in the vicinity;
- monitoring the temperature/humidity to ensure that precautions are effective.

Guidance 6

167 Asbestos removal and work in elevated temperatures are a difficult combination to manage and control effectively. Working in high temperatures can also lead to rapid deterioration in asbestos controls. All avenues should be explored to remove the heat source, including providing alternative plant. In particular, the various precautions needed to protect workers from exposure to asbestos dust and prevent its spread can cause a greatly increased temperature/thermal health risk.

168 Where elevated temperatures are caused by environmental conditions only (eg radiant heat or direct sunlight), the risk assessment should identify the measures that can be taken to reduce or eliminate the thermal risk. For example, scheduling the work to take place at other, cooler times, putting in place arrangements to shade the work area from sunlight; and/or additional air-cooling provisions.

169 The conditions must be monitored and where elevated temperatures occur while work is being done because of sudden changes in the weather (eg hot/sunny periods), or planned precautions are not effective, then the risk assessment should be reviewed and appropriate actions taken to control the risk.

170 Further information is available in *Asbestos: The licensed contractors' guide.*[9]

ACOP 6

Hot work

171 Hot work (ie work on hot plant and equipment) will only be permitted in exceptional and fully justifiable circumstances.

Guidance 6

172 Wherever possible, hot plant should be shut down or turned off and allowed to cool before asbestos removal work begins. Hot work is notifiable to HSE and is likely to be challenged during notification.

173 Work on hot plant (including pipework) can often be avoided by effective planning and organising, such as doing the work during scheduled maintenance shutdowns or holiday periods. Where work is required at short notice because of incidents or emergencies, take short-term remedial action as far as possible (eg by making temporary repairs or encapsulation) until further work can be incorporated into a programmed plant shut-down and carried out with the plant cold.

174 There may be some rare and exceptional circumstances where work on hot plant cannot be avoided (eg sudden or acute emergencies in health care premises). Where this is the case, a thorough and comprehensive risk assessment is needed and a well planned and designed control regime implemented.

175 Further information is available in *The licensed contractors' guide*.

ACOP 6

Reviewing assessments

176 Employers should review risk assessments as part of the ongoing management of their health and safety systems to make sure they are still relevant and reflect any lessons learned from what has gone well and what has not. A competent person should conduct the review. A specific review should take place if:

- **methods used to control fibre release change;**
- **there is doubt about the efficiency of control measures;**
- **there is a significant change in the type of work, amount of asbestos found or method of work;**
- **the results of air monitoring indicate the exposure levels to be higher than previously assessed.**

177 Where monitoring of exposure levels, or other information gathered during the course of work indicates that the initial assessment was wrong about either the duration of the task or nature of the materials:

- **immediately review the assessment and control measures and whether the nature and extent of the exposure means that the work should be done using different methods and equipment;**
- **review whether the work needs to be done by a licensed contractor;**
- **record any changes made to the risk assessment (the revised assessment must be available on site at all times).**

Regulation 7 Plans of work

Summary

This regulation requires employers to prepare a written plan before work on asbestos is carried out, including details of the work, and the appropriate actions to control risk and prevent harm.

Regulation 7

(1) An employer must not undertake any work with asbestos without having prepared a suitable written plan of work detailing how that work is to be carried out.

(2) The employer shall keep a copy of the plan of work at those premises at which the work to which the plan relates is being carried out for such time as that work continues.

(3) In cases of final demolition or major refurbishment of premises, the plan of work must, so far as is reasonably practicable, specify that asbestos must be removed before any other major works begin, unless removal would cause a greater risk to employees than if the asbestos had been left in place.

(4) The plan of work must include in particular details of—

(a) the nature and probable duration of the work;
(b) the location of the place where the work is to be carried out;
(c) the methods to be applied where the work involves the handling of asbestos or materials containing asbestos;
(d) the characteristics of the equipment to be used for—
(i) protection and decontamination of those carrying out the work, and
(ii) protection of other persons on or near the worksite;
(e) the measures which the employer intends to take in order to comply with the requirements of regulation 11; and
(f) the measures which the employer intends to take in order to comply with the requirements of regulation 17.

(5) The employer must ensure, so far as is reasonably practicable, that the work to which the plan of work relates is carried out in accordance with that plan and any subsequent written changes to it.

ACOP 7

178 For any work involving asbestos, including maintenance and survey work that may disturb it, the employer must draw up a written plan of how the work is to be carried out before it starts. Employers must make sure their employees follow the plan of work (sometimes called a method statement, plan, or POW) so far as reasonably practicable.

179 Where unacceptable risks to health and/or safety are discovered while work is in progress, eg disturbing hidden, missed or incorrectly identified ACMs, stop any work affecting the asbestos, except to put suitable controls in place and prevent further spread.

180 Where there is extensive damage to ACMs which causes contamination of the premises, or part of the premises, the area should be immediately evacuated. Work should not restart until a new plan of work is drawn up or until the existing plan is amended. Some measures may need to be carried out by licensed contractors.

ACOP 7

Contents

181 The plan of work must include the following information:

- **the nature and probable duration of the work;**
- **the number of people involved in the work;**
- **the address and location where the work is to be carried out;**
- **the methods to be used to prevent or reduce exposure to asbestos, eg prevention and control measures, arrangements for keeping premises and plant clean and arrangements for the handling and disposal of asbestos waste;**
- **the type of equipment, including PPE and RPE, used for:**
  - **protecting and decontaminating those carrying out the work;**
  - **protecting other people present at or near the worksite.**

182 Where necessary, the plan should include the site layout, a description of the location and nature of the asbestos present and which ACMs will be disturbed by the work.

183 Arrangements should be made to ensure that work is carried out in accordance with the plan of work, and any subsequent changes made to it.

184 Planning is a key requirement for all work with asbestos. The plan of work should be a practical and useful document, describing a safe working method for site staff to follow.

185 Plans of work should be drawn up by a suitably competent person.

Guidance 7

186 The plan must clearly describe how disturbance and spread of asbestos will be minimised or prevented.

187 A suitable and sufficient plan must be in a style and format that is easy for employees to use. Diagrams, flow charts, photographs and similar are very useful. The information about removal methods, controls and containment needs to be specified, so that it can act as a quick reference guide for those on site.

188 Generic information about frequently used company procedures will not need to be in the site-specific plan. Such information may form part of general procedures or health and safety policy documents and should be available on site for reference.

189 The plan of work should be suitable for the scale and type of work to be carried out.

ACOP 7

Demolition work

190 In the case of demolition or major refurbishment, the plan of work must specify that all asbestos is removed before any other major work begins, where this is reasonably practicable and does not cause a greater risk to employees than if the asbestos had been left in place.

Guidance 7

191 Where removal of ACMs is time-consuming and resource-intensive and only involves lower-risk material such as textured decorative coatings containing asbestos, then removal before demolition or major refurbishment may not be reasonably practicable.

ACOP 7

Licensable work

192 Suitable and sufficient plans of work are a licence condition for any licensable work with asbestos and a legal requirement. The plan of work is a critical element of management control.

193 It is a condition of the licence for licensed contractors to notify the appropriate enforcing authority at least 14 days before each job. A suitable and sufficient plan of work must have been prepared by the time of notification. If a suitable and sufficient plan is not available at the time of notification, the notification will be considered invalid and rejected by the enforcing authority.

Guidance 7

Purpose of the plan of work

194 The suitable and sufficient plan of work will be a practical and useful document, describing a safe working method for employees to follow.

195 It is an essential tool for senior managers/directors. It shows that they have considered significant site risks (asbestos and otherwise) and produced a specific job plan to address them.

Who creates the plan

196 The plan should be drawn up by a suitably competent person, following a visit and full appraisal of the site. Thorough discussions with others, such as the building owner, or dutyholder under regulation 4 of the Regulations, are an important part of the planning process. The most effective planning will involve input from employees, ie the operational staff who carry out/directly supervise the asbestos work.

How the plan of work is used

197 The plan is the record of how senior managers/directors want the job to be done. Its main purpose is to guide site work and an up-to-date copy must always be on site. A copy should also be kept at the head office, so management can effectively monitor performance. Access to general procedures should also be available at site level, either as paper copies or electronically. The plan should be kept updated to reflect any subsequent changes to the work.

198 Unnecessarily lengthy and complicated documents are not required. The plan needs to guide employees in a practical way on the work in hand.

Format and content

199 Plans should include the following:

- details of the scope of the work;
- relevant details from the contract for the work;
- equipment, materials and controls;
- other relevant site-specific information;
- method of work;
- management arrangements.

200 Further information on the detailed requirements for the plans of work for licensable work with asbestos can be found on the Asbestos Licensing Group pages on the HSE website at www.hse.gov.uk/aboutus/meetings/committees/alg.

ACOP 7

Communicating the plan of work

201 Work must not take place unless a copy of the plan of work is readily available on site. Employees must be informed of the contents of the plan and be instructed on the work methods and controls to use.

202 The plan of work must also be shown to anyone who needs to see it, including those carrying out the visual inspection and/or air clearance monitoring, once the work or section of work has ended.

203 Employers must make a copy of the plan of work available on request to employees, safety representatives and other elected representatives of employee health and safety, as well as others who may be affected by the work.

Regulation 8 Licensing of work with asbestos

Summary

This regulation requires employers to obtain a licence from HSE before they can carry out any licensable work with asbestos.

Regulation 8

(1) An employer must hold a licence granted under paragraph (2) before undertaking any licensable work with asbestos.

(2) The Executive may grant a licence for licensable work with asbestos if it considers it appropriate to do so and:

- *(a) the person who wishes to be granted the licence has made an application for it on a form approved for the purposes of this regulation by the Executive; and*
- *(b) the application was made at least 28 days before the date from which the licence is to run, or such shorter period as the Executive may allow.*

(3) A licence under this regulation—

- *(a) comes into operation on the date specified in the licence, and is valid for any period up to a maximum of three years that the Executive may specify in it; and*
- *(b) may be granted subject to such conditions as the Executive may consider appropriate.*

(4) The Executive may vary the terms of a licence under this regulation if it considers it appropriate to do so and in particular may—

- *(a) add further conditions and vary or omit existing ones; and*
- *(b) reduce the period for which the licence is valid or extend that period up to a maximum of three years from the date on which the licence first came into operation.*

(5) The Executive may revoke a licence if it considers it appropriate to do so.

(6) The holder of a licence under this regulation must return the licence to the Executive-

- *(a) when required by the Executive for any amendment; or*
- *(b) following its revocation.*

Guidance 8

204 Licensing allows HSE to make sure that those employers carrying out higher risk work on asbestos are able to demonstrate that they have the necessary knowledge, experience and expertise to adequately protect the health and safety of their employees and themselves and that they are competent to carry out the work.

205 Licensable work is work that meets the definition of 'licensable work with asbestos' set out in regulation 2 of the Regulations.

Applying for a licence

206 Licences are issued by HSE. HSE can set and amend terms and conditions of licences or revoke a licence. All licences are issued for a limited period (but are renewable) so that HSE can regularly review performance. Information on how to apply for a licence and the licensing procedure itself is provided in the *Asbestos licence assessment, amendment and revocation guide (ALAARG).*[10]

Appeals

207 Informal representations, in writing, against a decision to refuse to grant or to either revoke or not to renew a licence can be made to the senior HSE manager directly responsible for the Asbestos Licensing Unit at:

Health and Safety Executive
59 Belford Road
Edinburgh
EH4 3UE

208 If the matter is still not resolved, an appeal can be made to the Secretary of State for Work and Pensions under section 44 of the HSW Act (note that a section 44 appeal can be made at any stage with or without an internal HSE review of the decision). Normally the Secretary of State will appoint a person with relevant legal and/or practical experience to hear the appeal. The appeal may be decided on the basis of written submissions, but if either the person making the appeal or HSE want to be heard, the person hearing the appeal will give them that opportunity.

209 Appeals against a decision should include:

- the name and address of the person making the appeal;
- a photocopy of the current licence;
- the grounds for the appeal.

210 The appeal should be sent to:

The Secretary of State for Work and Pensions
Department for Work and Pensions (DWP)
Caxton House
Tothill Street
London SW1H 9NA

211 Further information on the appeals procedure is provided in *Asbestos licence assessment and revocation guide (ALAARG).*

Penalties

212 A conviction in the Crown Court/High Court or Sheriff Court on indictment for carrying out work without a licence or for breaching a term or condition attached to a licence, can result in an unlimited fine, imprisonment for a term of up to two years, or both.

Regulation 9 Notification of work with asbestos

Summary

This regulation requires employers to notify the appropriate enforcing authority of proposed work which is either licensable (always notifiable) or NNLW (applies to some non-licensable work). It also outlines the requirements to notify any material change which might affect the particulars of the original notification, this is particularly important for licensable work.

Regulation 9

(1) For licensable work with asbestos, an employer must notify the appropriate enforcing authority of—

(a) the particulars specified in Schedule 1 in writing at least 14 days (or such shorter time before as the appropriate enforcing authority may agree) before undertaking any licensable work with asbestos; and
(b) any material change, which might affect the particulars notified in accordance with (1)(a) (including the cessation of the work), in writing and without delay.

(2) For work with asbestos which is not licensable work with asbestos and is not exempted by regulation 3(2), an employer must notify the appropriate enforcing authority of-

(a) the particulars specified in Schedule 1, before work is commenced; and
(b) any material change, which might affect the particulars notified in accordance with (2)(a), without delay.

Guidance 9

213 The way work is notified differs depending if it is licensable or NNLW. For NNLW the process is simpler.

ACOP 9

Notification of licensable work

214 When undertaking licensable work, the appropriate enforcing authority must be notified with details of the proposed work at least 14 days before work starts. This enables the authority to assess the proposals for carrying out work with asbestos and if appropriate, to inspect the site either before or during the work.

Guidance 9

215 Although the requirement is to notify the relevant enforcing authority office in writing at least 14 days before any licensable work begins, the enforcing authority may allow a shorter period, eg in an emergency where there is a serious risk to the health and safety of any person. This shorter period is known as a 'waiver' or 'dispensation'.

216 Normally each individual licensable job should be notified to the enforcing authority. Table 7 provides information about which enforcing authority to send the notification to. However, a single notification of licensable asbestos work may be submitted to the enforcing authority for work likely to be regularly repeated on the same premises. If there are several premises, a separate notification is required for each of them. Any other subsequent work not covered in the original notification will need to be separately notified.

ACOP 9

217 The enforcing authority should be informed in writing if there are changes to the work that might affect the particulars of the notification.

Guidance 9

218 The notification form FOD ASB5[11] is available from the HSE website, local HSE offices or from the Asbestos Licensing Unit.

219 Licensable work can be notified by telephone to the enforcing authority, especially if there is uncertainty about which authority to notify. However, this must be followed up by confirmation in writing or on form FOD ASB5 to the relevant enforcing authority at least 14 days before the work starts.

Table 7 How to identify the appropriate enforcing authority

Type of premises/activity	Enforcing Authority
Shops, offices, separate catering services, launderettes, sport, entertainment and recreational activities, exhibitions, church or religious meetings, hotels, camping and caravan sites, wholesale and retail storage	LA (local authority)
Factories and factory offices, civil engineering, construction and demolition sites, hospitals, research and development establishments, local government services and educational establishments, fairgrounds, radio, television and film broadcasting, seagoing ships, docks, transport undertakings, domestic premises, quarries, farms (and associated activities), horticultural premises and forestries, mines/quarries and offshore installations, licensed nuclear sites	HSE (Health and Safety Executive)
Railways, railway lines, signal boxes	ORR (Office of Rail Regulation)

ACOP 9

Notification of NNLW

220 Employers who plan to carry out NNLW should notify the work using the online notification form for notifying all the relevant authorities. Notification must be made before the work begins.

221 Notifications can only be made using the online notification form ASB NNLW1.[12]

Guidance 9

222 All three enforcing authorities (HSE, local authorities and ORR) can be notified using the online notification form. Dutyholders should be aware that:

- notification should take place before work starts, but there is no stipulated minimum prior notice period;
- work may proceed once notification has been submitted, no permission for work to proceed is required;
- an acknowledgment PDF copy of your notification will be provided electronically and should be kept with other documentation (such as the plan of work) relating to the activity;
- for a long-term project of work involving multiple jobs in one localised area (eg a housing estate or large commercial premises) the whole project should be notified once;

Guidance 9

- licensed asbestos contractors are required to notify both licensable and NNLW work.

223 There is further guidance on the online notification form itself.

224 The decision as to whether it is NNLW or not may in certain cases depend entirely on the condition of the ACM on site and will be a matter of judgement and opinion. A person with sufficient experience and knowledge, who has been trained according to regulation 10, and who will be able to show their decision was reasonable, should make the decision.

Regulation 10 Information, instruction and training

Summary

This regulation requires employers to make sure that anyone liable to disturb asbestos during their work, or who supervises such employees, receives the correct level of information, instruction and training to enable them to carry out their work safely and competently and without risk to themselves or others.

Regulation 10

(1) Every employer must ensure that any employee employed by that employer is given adequate information, instruction and training where that employee—

(a) is or is liable to be exposed to asbestos, or if that employee supervises such employees, so that those employees are aware of—
  - *(i) the properties of asbestos and its effects on health, including its interaction with smoking,*
  - *(ii) the types of products or materials likely to contain asbestos,*
  - *(iii) the operations which could result in asbestos exposure and the importance of preventive controls to minimise exposure,*
  - *(iv) safe work practices, control measures, and protective equipment,*
  - *(v) the purpose, choice, limitations, proper use and maintenance of respiratory protective equipment,*
  - *(vi) emergency procedures,*
  - *(vii) hygiene requirements,*
  - *(viii) decontamination procedures,*
  - *(ix) waste handling procedures,*
  - *(x) medical examination requirements, and*
  - *(xi) the control limit and the need for air monitoring,*

in order to safeguard themselves and other employees; and

(b) carries out work in connection with the employer's duties under these Regulations, so that the employee can carry out that work effectively.

(2) The information, instruction and training required by paragraph (1) must be—

(a) given at regular intervals;
(b) adapted to take account of significant changes in the type of work carried out or methods of work used by the employer; and
(c) provided in a manner appropriate to the nature and degree of exposure identified by the risk assessment, and so that the employees are aware of—
  - *(i) the significant findings of the risk assessment, and*
  - *(ii) the results of any air monitoring carried out with an explanation of the findings.*

ACOP 10

Information, instruction and training for all work with asbestos

225 Employers have a duty to ensure that the information, instruction and training given to their employees is adequate to allow them to safeguard themselves and other employees and to carry out their work with asbestos effectively.

Competence

226 Any reference to competence, competent persons or competent employees in relation to working with asbestos is a reference to a person or employee who has received adequate information, instruction and training for the task being done and can demonstrate an adequate and up-to-date understanding of the work, required control measures and appropriate law. They must also have enough experience to apply this knowledge effectively.

Guidance 10

227 A training course on its own will not make an employee competent. Competence is developed over time by implementing and consolidating skills learnt during training, on-the-job learning, instruction and assessment.

228 It is essential for recently trained employees, particularly those new to asbestos-related work, to consolidate their newly acquired skills and knowledge by putting them to use on the job as soon as possible. Employers, supervisors and managers will play an important role in coaching new employees by reinforcing good work practices and correcting bad ones. Where persistent problems occur, retraining may be required. Further training can then be tailored to deal with performance weakness and gaps in relevant skills.

229 Similarly, longstanding employees may benefit from reassessment and a skills update.

ACOP 10

230 There are three main types of information, instruction and training. These relate to:

- **asbestos awareness;**
- **non-licensable work with asbestos including NNLW;**
- **licensable work with asbestos.**

Guidance 10

231 All information, instruction and training given should include an appropriate level of detail, be suitable to the work being done, and use written materials, oral presentation and practical demonstration as necessary.

ACOP 10

Asbestos awareness

232 Asbestos awareness training should be given to employees whose work could foreseeably disturb the fabric of a building and expose them to asbestos or who supervise or influence the work.

233 In particular, it should be given to those workers in the refurbishment, maintenance and allied trades where it is foreseeable that ACMs may become exposed during their work. This includes, but is not limited to:

- **demolition workers;**
- **construction workers;**
- **general maintenance staff;**
- **electricians;**
- **plumbers;**

ACOP 10

- **gas fitters;**
- **painters and decorators;**
- **joiners;**
- **shop fitters;**
- **plasterers;**
- **roofers;**
- **heating and ventilation engineers;**
- **telecommunication engineers;**
- **computer and data installers;**
- **fire and burglar alarm installers;**
- **architects, building surveyors and other such professionals.**

234 This requirement does not apply where the employer can demonstrate that work will only be carried out in or on premises free of ACMs. This information should be available as a result of the assessment made by the dutyholder under the duty to manage in regulation 4 and the duty on the employer to identify the presence of asbestos in regulation 5.

235 Asbestos awareness training should cover the following topics:

- **the properties of asbestos and its effects on health, including the increased risk of lung cancer for asbestos workers who smoke;**
- **the types, uses and likely occurrence of asbestos and ACMs in buildings and plant;**
- **the general procedures to be followed to deal with an emergency, eg an uncontrolled release of asbestos dust into the workplace;**
- **how to avoid the risks from asbestos, eg for building work, no employee should carry out work which disturbs the fabric of a building unless the employer has confirmed that ACMs are not present.**

Guidance 10

236 Asbestos awareness will not prepare employees or self-employed contractors to carry out work with ACMs. Awareness training is only intended to help employees avoid carrying out work that will disturb asbestos or ACMs.

ACOP 10

237 If work is planned that will disturb ACMs, further information, instruction and training appropriate to the work being done will be needed.

Non-licensable work including NNLW

238 In addition to the 'asbestos awareness' in paragraph 235, those employees whose work will knowingly disturb ACMs, and which is defined as non-licensable work or NNLW, should receive additional task-specific information, instruction and training.

Guidance 10

239 The procedures for providing information, instruction and training for non-licensable work with asbestos should be clearly defined and referred to in a written health and safety policy document. This should be reviewed regularly, particularly when work methods change. Records should be kept of each individual's training.

ACOP 10

Provision of information

240 For those employees doing non-licensable work with asbestos, employers should make the following information available for the current work being done:

- **a copy of the risk assessment for that work;**
- **a copy of the plan of work;**
- **where applicable, details of any air monitoring and results.**

ACOP 10

241 In addition, the following information should be made available to workers, on request:

- maintenance records for control measures;
- personal information from health records (ie relating to NNLW and only to the individual employee concerned);
- the results of any face-fit test (FFT) for RPE provided for work with asbestos;
- a copy of the individual's training record.

Guidance 10

242 Training needs analysis (TNA) will help identify which of the topics listed below should be covered to ensure the level of competency needed to avoid workers putting themselves or others at risk in the course of their duties.

ACOP 10

Training for non-licensable work

243 Training for non-licensable work should include information on:

- the operations which could result in asbestos exposure and the importance of preventive controls to minimise exposure;
- how to make suitable and sufficient assessments of the risk of exposure to asbestos;
- the control limit, and the purpose of air monitoring;
- safe work practices, control measures, and protective equipment. This should include an explanation of how the correct use and maintenance of control measures, protective equipment and work methods can reduce the risks from asbestos, limit exposure to workers and limit the spread of asbestos fibres outside the work area including, where relevant, the maintenance of enclosures;
- procedures for recording, reporting and correcting defects;
- the purpose, appropriate choice and correct selection from a range of suitable RPE, including any limitations;
- the correct use, and where relevant, cleaning, maintenance and safe storage of RPE and PPE, in accordance with the manufacturer's instructions and information;
- the importance of achieving and maintaining a good seal between face and RPE, the relevance of pre-use tests and FFTs, and the importance of being clean-shaven;
- hygiene requirements;
- requirements and procedures for medical examination, for NNLW;
- decontamination procedures;
- waste handling procedures;
- emergency procedures, including how to deal with an emergency release;
- which work requires notification as NNLW and which work requires an HSE licence;
- an introduction to the relevant regulations, ACOPs and guidance that apply to asbestos work and other regulations that deal with the carriage and disposal of asbestos;
- personal sampling and leak and clearance sampling techniques, for analysts;
- other work hazards, including working at height, electrical, slips, trips and falls, where this is applicable to the work being done.

Practical training for non-licensable work

244 Where any employees are required to use plant and equipment or carry out the following work activities, practical training should be given (ie the

ACOP 10

opportunity to try and practice for themselves, in addition to having it explained or demonstrated to them):

- use of decontamination facilities;
- use of PPE, particularly RPE;
- construction of mini-enclosures where necessary;
- use of control techniques, such as class H vacuum cleaners (BS 8520-3:2009).

Record keeping for employees carrying out non-licensable work, including NNLW

245 A record of the information, instruction and training received by each individual for non-licensable work should be kept to:

- help employers carry out ongoing TNA;
- support individual workers in demonstrating their knowledge, skills and experience when they move from one employer to another.

Licensable work

246 In addition to the 'asbestos awareness' in paragraph 235 those employees carrying out work defined as 'licensable work' should receive additional task-specific information, instruction and training.

Guidance 10

247 *The licensed contractors' guide* sets out the detailed content of the asbestos training modules for operatives, supervisors, managers and directors involved in licensable work.

ACOP 10

Providing information

248 Employers should make the information in paragraphs 249–250 available to employees doing licensable work with asbestos.

249 For the specific work being done:

- a copy of the risk assessment for that work;
- a copy of the plan of work;
- details of any air monitoring and results;
- details of notification under regulation 9 made to the enforcing authority.

250 More general information:

- maintenance records for control measures;
- personal information from health records (only relating to the individual employee concerned);
- the results of any FFT for RPE provided for work with asbestos;
- a copy of the licence;
- any anonymised collective information from the health records.

Training for licensable work

251 Training given to employees (including operatives, supervisors, managers, directors) doing licensable work with asbestos should include:

- the health risks to employees' families and others from taking home contaminated equipment and clothing and the increased risk of lung cancer for asbestos workers who smoke;
- the risk assessment and the purpose of the plan of work;

ACOP 10

- the operations which could result in asbestos exposure and the importance of preventive controls to minimise exposure;
- the control limit, assessment of exposure and the purpose and importance of air monitoring to check compliance with the limit, including the purpose of personal sampling;
- safe work practices, control measures, and protective equipment, including an explanation of how the correct use of control measures, protective equipment and work methods can reduce the risks from asbestos, limit exposure to workers and limit the spread of asbestos fibres outside the work area;
- the importance of following the procedures, controls and preventative measures set out in the plan of work and risk assessment;
- the maintenance of control measures including, where relevant, enclosures and negative pressure equipment;
- procedures for recording, reporting and correcting defects in control measures, protective equipment and work methods;
- the purpose, appropriate choice and correct selection from a range of suitable RPE, including any limitations;
- the correct use, cleaning, maintenance and safe storage of RPE, with specific attention to make sure RPE is working correctly, in accordance with the manufacturer's instructions and information;
- the importance of achieving and maintaining a good seal between face and RPE, the relevance of fit tests, and the importance of being clean shaven;
- the suitability, correct use, storage and maintenance of protective clothing, including clothing used for transit;
- hygiene requirements;
- decontamination procedures, particularly within enclosures, airlocks (including bag locks) and hygiene units;
- site set-up: marking out the work area, setting up barriers, transit routes and waste storage area, pre-cleaning, sealing sources of potential leaks, construction and layout of the enclosure, including negative pressure units, viewing panels and airlocks, positioning of decontamination units, air management and leak testing;
- controlled removal techniques and how they work, including types of wet surfactant, injection of sprayed asbestos and lagging, spray wetting of AIB and asbestos cement, the wrap-and-cut technique, and (if relevant) the use of glove bags;
- waste handling procedures including bagging, storage and disposal;
- site clean-up and clearance procedures, including the certificate of reoccupation arrangements;
- emergency procedures, including general procedures, such as the uncontrolled release of asbestos fibres into the workplace or outbreak of fire;
- requirements and procedures for medical examination;
- the results of any air monitoring, carried out with an explanation of the findings;
- other work hazards, including working at height, electrical, slips, trips and falls;
- an introduction to the relevant regulations, ACOPs and guidance that apply to asbestos work and other regulations that deal with the carriage and disposal of asbestos.

Supervisors, managers and directors

252 To help employers comply with their legal duties under the Regulations, additional training, at an appropriate level, should be given to supervisors,

ACOP 10

managers and directors, so that they can effectively carry out their role on site. This should include:

- their responsibilities for directing, supervising and monitoring all aspects of work on site, including health and safety, particularly the importance of making sure employees and others follow the procedures, controls and preventative measures set out in the plan of work and risk assessment;
- the importance of the supervisor being on site at all key stages of the work (witnessing the smoke test, ensuring that the hygiene facilities are fully operational before work starts, ensuring signs and barriers are correctly erected, carrying out daily checks) to ensure that it is done safely;
- how to produce and implement plans of work that set out the appropriate procedures, controls and preventative measures based on the assessment, including how and when to update plans of work;
- how and when to notify the appropriate enforcing authorities that work is taking place and about situations where re-notification is necessary;
- how to deal with situations where the methods set out in the plan of work cannot be followed, due to a change in circumstances and a revision to the plan is needed;
- the application of suitable emergency procedures if controls fail;
- the importance of monitoring and auditing the work activities;
- the importance of having effective arrangements in place to communicate with and monitor workers inside the enclosure and hygiene unit;
- the need to provide additional training, information and instruction to workers as necessary, such as in the use of a particular piece of equipment or work method, which they have not previously trained in;
- how to assess the competence of employees and identify their training needs;
- when and how to do air monitoring, how the results are interpreted and who needs to see them;
- how the results and records of personal air sampling, fit tests and medicals should be kept and maintained and who needs to see them;
- how to apply the procedures for dealing with accidents, incidents and emergencies;
- the importance of keeping the work area clean and free of asbestos;
- the importance of making sure the correct procedures are followed at the end of the job to allow a certificate of reoccupation to be issued;
- an understanding of what the laboratory analyst will require before doing clearance sampling and issuing the certificate of reoccupation.

Practical training for licensable work

253 Practical training is essential for those entering enclosures, including employees and supervisors. Where employees are required to use the following plant and equipment, or carry out the following work activities or procedures, they also need practical training in the:

- decontamination procedures and use of hygiene facilities;
- use of PPE, particularly RPE;
- construction of enclosures, airlocks and achieving sufficient numbers of air changes within the enclosure;
- controlled removal techniques, including the use of multiple and single needle injection systems, glovebags and wrap-and-cut techniques;
- waste removal procedures on site, including double bagging and removal through the bag lock.

ACOP 10

Record-keeping for employees carrying out licensable work
254 A record of the information, instruction and training received by each individual for licensable work should be kept to:

- **help employers carry out ongoing TNA;**
- **comply with the licensing process, where applicable;**
- **support individual workers in demonstrating their knowledge, skills and experience when they move from one employer to another.**

Guidance 10

255 The procedures for providing information, instruction and training for licensable work should be clearly defined and referred to in a written document. Employers should review this regularly, particularly when work methods change.

ACOP 10

Competence in respirator zones
256 Employers carrying out licensable work in a respirator zone must make sure that only competent employees enter that respirator zone, or supervise such employees.

257 To comply with the requirements in regulation 18(4)(a) and (b), employers must be able to demonstrate that operatives and supervisors have been given adequate information, instruction and training.

Competence of those providing training
258 All training should be given by people who are competent to do so and who have personal practical experience and a theoretical knowledge of all relevant aspects of the work being carried out by the employer.

Duration of training

259 The duration of training should be appropriate to:

- **the type of training (whether initial training or refresher training);**
- **the role for which the person is being trained;**
- **the nature of the work (non-licensable work, NNLW and licensable work with asbestos).**

Training for examination and test methods and techniques

260 Anyone who carries out any examination, testing (including clearance inspection, air monitoring and exposure monitoring) or maintenance of plant or equipment (eg LEV systems and RPE) should have sufficient training and experience in examination and test methods and techniques to ensure that they are competent.

Provision of information and training for safety representatives

261 Training for safety representatives and elected representatives of employee safety needs to be appropriate to their role.

262 Employers should consult safety representatives and elected representatives of employee safety in good time about the information, instruction and training they intend to provide.

263 Where the results of air monitoring show that the relevant control limit has been unexpectedly exceeded, employers should tell employees, safety representatives and elected representatives of employee health and safety about this as quickly as possible and give details of the reasons for what happened and the action taken or proposed.

ACOP 10

Refresher training

Refresher training for licensable and non-licensable work

264 Employers should identify the specific training needs of their employees so that the refresher training can be appropriately tailored to the licensable or non-licensable work being done. It should reflect the level of competence and specific training needs of the individual involved and should not be a repeat of the initial information, instruction and training.

Guidance 10

265 Refresher training for licensable and non-licensable work should be appropriate to the work the individual is doing. It should be based on a TNA which will inform the type of training needed. For example, for those with extensive training needs, refresher training may involve classroom teaching or practical training but for others, it could be given as part of other health and safety updates, eg as part of a short toolbox talk or e-learning to refresh experienced workers on the main principles and expectations.

ACOP 10

266 Refresher training for licensable and non-licensable work should be given every year, or more frequently if:

- **work methods change;**
- **the type of equipment used to control exposure changes;**
- **the type of work carried out changes significantly; or**
- **gaps in competency are identified.**

267 It should include reviewing where things have gone wrong and sharing good practice.

268 Where training needs dictate, refresher training should include an appropriate element of practical training, particularly covering decontamination procedures, use of RPE, FFT and controlled removal techniques.

Guidance 10

Refresher asbestos awareness training

269 There is no need for employees who receive training for licensable or non-licensable work to do asbestos awareness refresher training.

270 Awareness training is only intended to help employees avoid carrying out work that will disturb asbestos. There is no legal requirement to repeat a formal refresher awareness training course every 12 months. However some form of refresher awareness should be given, as necessary, to help prevent those workers listed in paragraph 233 putting themselves or others at risk in the course of their work.

271 Refresher awareness could be given as e-learning or as part of other health and safety updates, rather than through a formal training course. For example, an employer, manager or supervisor who has attended an awareness course and is competent to do so, as defined in paragraph 258, could deliver an update or safety talk to employees in house.

272 A realistic, common sense approach to refreshing knowledge and skills, based on judgement of individual abilities and training needs, is all that is usually required.

ACOP 10

Information and instruction for non-employees

273 Employers who are working on asbestos in premises have a duty to make sure, so far as is reasonably practicable, that adequate information and instruction is given to those not employed by them, who are present in the premises and could be affected by the work.

ACOP 10

274 The information provided should include details of:

- **the location(s) where work is taking place, so people can avoid them;**
- **possible risks from rearranging thoroughfares and fire exits as a result of the work being done;**
- **any other information to help people avoid risks from the disturbance of ACMs caused by the work being done.**

Guidance 10

Certificates of training

275 There is no legal requirement for employees to be issued with or possess a certificate of training before they can work with asbestos. However, many external training providers issue trainees with certificates to indicate completion of a training course. A certificate is not proof of competency to do the job, but where issued, a certificate is an indication that training has been received and may be kept as part of an individual's training record.

Regulation 11 Prevention or reduction of exposure to asbestos

Summary

This regulation requires employers to prevent employees being exposed to asbestos or, if this is not possible, to put in place the measures and controls necessary to reduce exposure to as low as is reasonably practicable.

Regulation 11

(1) Every employer must—

(a) prevent the exposure to asbestos of any employee employed by that employer so far as is reasonably practicable;

(b) where it is not reasonably practicable to prevent such exposure—

(i) take the measures necessary to reduce exposure to asbestos of any such employee to the lowest level reasonably practicable by measures other than the use of respiratory protective equipment, and

(ii) ensure that the number of any such employees exposed to asbestos at any one time is as low as is reasonably practicable.

(2) Where it is not reasonably practicable for the employer to prevent the exposure to asbestos of any such employee employed by that employer in accordance with paragraph (1)(a), the measures referred to in paragraph (1)(b)(i) must include, in order of priority—

(a) the design and use of appropriate work processes, systems and engineering controls and the provision and use of suitable work equipment and materials in order to avoid or minimise the release of asbestos; and

(b) the control of exposure at source, including adequate ventilation systems and appropriate organisational measures,

and the employer must so far as is reasonably practicable provide any employee concerned with suitable respiratory protective equipment in addition to the measures required by sub-paragraphs (a) and (b).

(3) Where it is not reasonably practicable for the employer to reduce the exposure to asbestos of any such employee to below the control limit by the

Regulation 11

measures referred to in paragraph (1)(b)(i), then, in addition to taking those measures, the employer must provide that employee with suitable respiratory protective equipment which will reduce the concentration of asbestos in the air inhaled by that employee (after taking account of the effect of that respiratory protective equipment) to a concentration which is—

(a) below the control limit; and
(b) as low as is reasonably practicable.

(4) Personal protective equipment provided by an employer in accordance with this regulation or with regulation 14(1) must be suitable for its purpose and—

(a) comply with any provision of the Personal Protective Equipment Regulations 2002 which is applicable to that item of personal protective equipment; or
(b) in the case of respiratory protective equipment, where no provision referred to in sub-paragraph (a) applies, be of a type approved or must conform to a standard approved, in either case, by the Executive.

(5) The employer must—

(a) ensure that no employee is exposed to asbestos in a concentration in the air inhaled by that worker which exceeds the control limit; or
(b) if the control limit is exceeded—
(i) immediately inform any employees concerned and their representatives and ensure that work does not continue in the affected area until adequate measures have been taken to reduce employees' exposure to asbestos below the control limit,
(ii) as soon as is reasonably practicable identify the reasons for the control limit being exceeded and take the appropriate measures to prevent it being exceeded again, and
(iii) check the effectiveness of the measures taken pursuant to sub-paragraph (ii) by carrying out immediate air monitoring.

ACOP 11

276 Employers must first decide whether they can prevent the exposure to asbestos so far as is reasonably practicable. If this is not possible then exposure must be reduced to as low as reasonably practicable.

277 Work which disturbs, or is liable to disturb ACMs, should only be carried out when it is unavoidable.

278 Where it is not reasonably practicable to prevent exposure to asbestos, it must first be reduced to the lowest level reasonably practicable, by means other than the use of RPE.

Guidance 11

279 It may be that the work which would disturb the asbestos or ACM is not necessary or that it can be carried out in an alternative way, which would not involve disturbing the asbestos, or would minimise such disturbance (eg re-routing cables away from ACMs or covering up materials, rather than working on them).

ACOP 11

280 Where it is not reasonably practicable to prevent exposure to asbestos, employers must choose the most effective method or combination of methods to minimise fibre release and reduce exposure to the lowest levels reasonably practicable. This must be documented in the written risk assessment and/or plan of work. Such work methods should include as appropriate:

ACOP 11

- **safe removal of ACMs before any other major work (such as refurbishment) begins, using the most effective methods to minimise fibre release (eg controlled wet stripping techniques);**
- **choosing methods that do not involve dry working and avoiding abrasion, sanding, machining or cutting etc of ACMs;**
- **choosing work methods with the least overall risk;**
- **where necessary, carrying out a pre-clean of the work area before removal work takes place, and a prompt clear-up at regular intervals, using vacuum-cleaning equipment of class H (BS 8520–3:2009) to clean up any dust and debris which may contain asbestos;**
- **not allowing waste to be kept on site for longer than necessary;**
- **removing an intact item instead of detaching ACM panelling attached to it;**
- **wrapping and cutting off or removing pipes at the flange joints, rather than disturbing the insulation material on them;**
- **re-routing cables and services away from ACMs;**
- **protecting ACMs from damage when working near them;**
- **cutting the bolts holding asbestos cement cladding or roofing sheets in place from a safe working platform and removing them whole.**

Guidance 11

281 When considering work methods, employers should be aware of other risks, not just those relating to asbestos exposure. For example asbestos cement corrugated roofing is highly fragile and should never be walked on directly. If work must be done on or over asbestos cement sheets, a safe system of work must be devised and used.

ACOP 11

282 Employers should keep the number of both employees and others who might be exposed to asbestos at any one time as low as reasonably practicable.

283 Employers should reduce airborne levels of asbestos to as low a level as reasonably practicable and control exposure, so that any peak exposure is less than 0.6 fibres per cm^3 averaged over a maximum continuous period of ten minutes. This should be done by using appropriate RPE, if exposure cannot be reduced sufficiently by other means.

Viewing panels and CCTV for enclosures

284 All areas of the enclosure should be able to be monitored during work activities and this should be achieved by a combination of viewing panels and/or CCTV. The quality of the CCTV system should ensure clear and distinct pictures.

Guidance 11

Non-licensable removal work

285 The duty to avoid, or if that is not reasonably practicable, adequately control, exposure applies equally to all work with asbestos, irrespective of whether a licence is required or not.

286 Employers should have in place a policy to always check whether ACMs are present before carrying out work that disturbs the fabric of a building which may contain asbestos. The policy should also ensure that work which does disturb ACMs is restricted to authorised people who have been given the necessary information, instruction and training. Also, non-licensable asbestos work should be carried out using the most effective method or combination of methods which minimises fibre release and so reduces exposure to the lowest levels reasonably practicable. Some examples of work methods which reduce dust emission are:

Guidance 11

- removing asbestos cement sheets whole;
- avoiding the use of power tools;
- keeping materials thoroughly wet;
- using LEV systems, such as cowls on drills and shadow vacuuming.

287 Further guidance on methods of working with asbestos cement products, minor works with building materials containing asbestos and on work with asbestos-containing textured decorative coatings, can be found in HSE's *Asbestos essentials* task sheets.

ACOP 11

Licensable removal work

288 Employers must choose work methods which are most effective at reducing fibre release at source.

Removing asbestos insulation and asbestos coating

289 For work with asbestos insulation and coating, this should involve controlled wet stripping and avoid the use of abrasive power tools.

Guidance 11

290 The standards in BS 8520-1:2009 on controlled wetting equipment specification should be followed.

291 There may, however, be situations where other techniques such as wrap-and-cut may be more efficient at preventing or reducing exposure (eg for removing redundant pipework).

ACOP 11

292 Where wet injection techniques are used, they should be used to uniformly wet the asbestos material before its removal. The wetting agent will need enough time to thoroughly penetrate the ACM, but saturation of the material should be avoided.

Guidance 11

293 Oversaturation can lead to pieces of ACM falling off and may turn the material into unmanageable slurry. It is essential that employers check the degree of saturation (eg by visual inspection, examining texture or by using dyes, before beginning removal). The treated ACM should have a dough-like consistency.

ACOP 11

294 Where the ACM is being removed from its substrate, employers must not use dry stripping methods unless there is no reasonably practicable alternative (eg stripping using a glovebag without any form of wetting is a dry method). The work method must be justified by the risk assessment and clearly detailed in the plan of work. Employers must make sure that effective measures are used to control fibre release in the work area (eg glovebags within the enclosure, vacuum transfer).

Guidance 11

295 Before agreeing to a request for the work to be carried out dry, licensed contractors should discuss this with the relevant enforcing authority.

296 Occupiers and owners of buildings and plant should co-operate with licensed contractors undertaking the work, releasing plant wherever practicable, so that it can be isolated and worked on cold and free from electrical and chemical risks.

297 More guidance on fibre control methods can be found in *The licensed contractors' guide*.

ACOP 11

Maintaining plant and equipment contaminated with asbestos

298 Where there is a risk of asbestos fibre release, all maintenance of equipment contaminated with asbestos must be done under controlled conditions. For example when an item of plant needs to be stripped down (such as air extraction equipment), it should be carried out within a work area, permanently set aside, which is under negative pressure and which is connected to the hygiene facilities by an airlock system. Where this work is done on site it must be done in an enclosure.

299 Employers should control dust-containing asbestos fibres at source by using LEV or controlled wetting techniques, eg airless or low-pressure spraying. Employers should take care not to overwater when working on or near electrical equipment or, alternatively, use dielectric fluids. Employees and others who carry out such maintenance work either on site or on the maintenance company's own premises will require a licence.

Respiratory protective equipment

300 Where, despite the use of other control measures, the assessment of the work concludes that exposure of workers is liable to exceed the control limit or exceed the 0.6 f/cm^3 peak level measured over 10 minutes, employers must provide suitable RPE. This must reduce exposure to a level as low as is reasonably practicable below the control limit. In addition, employers should make sure that RPE is used correctly by those carrying out the work. RPE should be examined before use. See paragraphs 337–344.

301 Exposure above the control limit also triggers the need for immediate steps under regulation 11(5) to inform employees and safety representatives and for respirator zones, required under regulation 18 (see paragraphs 469–478).

302 RPE must be matched to:

- the job;
- the environment;
- the anticipated maximum exposure;
- the wearer (and take into account such issues as facial hair and glasses).

303 RPE should be compatible with any other PPE. In particular, any PPE which protects the head or eyes of employees should not affect the fit of the RPE.

304 Employers should make sure that the selected facepiece (tight and loose-fitting types) is the right size and can correctly fit the wearer. For a tight-fitting facepiece (disposable masks, half-face masks and full-face masks) the initial selection should include fit testing to make sure the wearer has equipment which fits correctly. Employers should have systems in place to make sure that face-fit testing is carried out and repeated as necessary on a regular basis. Employers should make sure that whoever carries out fit testing is competent to do so.

305 Repeat fit testing must be done when changing to a different model of RPE, or a different sized facepiece or if there have been significant changes to the facial characteristics of the individual wearer, eg as a result of significant weight gain or weight loss or due to dentistry.

Guidance 11

306 It is good practice to have a system in place to ensure repeat fit testing of RPE is carried out regularly, eg annual testing for workers involved in licensed asbestos removal.

307 Where RPE is required, employers should choose RPE designed to protect against exposures well above those expected, to allow for unexpected high exposures and to provide an adequate margin of safety. If there is doubt about the level of protection, employers should always select higher performance equipment, provided it is suitable for the work.

308 For licensable work inside enclosures, power-assisted full-facepiece respirators fitted with P3 filters should be worn. Alternatively, similar or higher performance equipment can be used, eg powered hoods or blouse or air-fed equipment. Disposable RPE (eg FFP3) or half-mask RPE (with P3 filters) can be used in low-risk ancillary tasks, as identified in the risk assessment. These situations could include scaffold erection, site set-up, enclosure dismantling, and waste handling outside the enclosure.

Fit testing facepieces

309 There is comprehensive information and guidance on face-fit testing of RPE at www.hse.gov.uk/respiratory-protective-equipment.

Regulation 12 Use of control measures etc

Summary

This regulation requires employers to put procedures in place to make sure employees use and apply control measures. It also requires the employees to make full and proper use of those measures.

Regulation 12

(1) Every employer who provides any control measure, other thing or facility pursuant to these Regulations must take all reasonable steps to ensure that it is properly used or applied as the case may be.

(2) Every employee must make full and proper use of any control measure, other thing or facility provided pursuant to these Regulations and—

(a) where relevant take all reasonable steps to ensure that it is returned after use to any accommodation provided for it; and
(b) report any defect discovered without delay to that employee's employer.

ACOP 12

310 Employers should have procedures in place to make sure control measures are used and applied properly and are not made less effective by other work practices or other machinery. These procedures should include:

- **regular checks, at least at the start of every shift;**
- **prompt action when a problem is identified.**

General duties on employees

311 Within the general duties imposed by regulation 12(2), employees should, in particular:

- **use any control measures properly and keep equipment in the places provided – this includes dust suppression, extraction equipment, RPE and protective clothing;**

ACOP 12

- carefully follow the procedures set out in the employer's risk assessment and plan of work, including those for changing and decontamination, and comply with the use of control measures;
- keep the workplace clean;
- eat, drink and smoke only in the designated places provided;
- report any defects concerning control measures to their supervisor/ manager immediately.

312 RPE should never be taken off and put down in a contaminated area, except in the case of a medical emergency. When not in use, RPE should not be:

- hung around the neck or in any other way allowed to come into contact with contaminated clothing;
- stored in a contaminated area.

313 RPE and protective clothing should be:

- removed at the end of each working period;
- cleaned (see paragraph 344 for RPE and paragraphs 357–363 for PPE);
- kept in the storage place provided specifically for that purpose which is clean and will protect it from damage.

314 Before it is used, disposable RPE should be kept in a suitable container to keep it free from contamination. Once it has been used, disposable RPE and protective clothing should be treated as asbestos waste.

Regulation 13 Maintenance of control measures etc

Summary

This regulation requires employers to carry out regular inspection and maintenance of control measures to make sure they are kept in good efficient working order. It also requires a competent person to test and examine exhaust ventilation and RPE at suitable intervals and for records of examinations and tests to be kept for at least five years.

Regulation 13

(1) Every employer who provides any control measure to meet the requirements of these Regulations must ensure that—

(a) in the case of plant and equipment, including engineering controls and personal protective equipment, it is maintained in an efficient state, in efficient working order, in good repair and in a clean condition; and

(b) in the case of provision of systems of work and supervision and of any other measure, any such measures are reviewed at suitable intervals and revised if necessary.

(2) Where exhaust ventilation equipment or respiratory protective equipment (except disposable respiratory protective equipment) is provided to meet the requirements of these Regulations, the employer must ensure that thorough examinations and tests of that equipment are carried out at suitable intervals by a competent person.

(3) Every employer must keep a suitable record of the examinations and tests carried out in accordance with paragraph (2) and of repairs carried out as a result of those examinations and tests, and that record or a suitable summary of it must be kept available for at least 5 years from the date on which it was made.

ACOP 13

315 Employers must draw up maintenance procedures for all control measures and PPE. These should also cover the equipment used for cleaning, washing and changing facilities and the controls used to prevent the spread of contamination. The procedures should make it clear which control measures require maintenance, when and how to carry this out and who is responsible for doing it. In particular, maintenance is required for:

- enclosures;
- hygiene facilities;
- vacuum cleaners;
- air extraction equipment;
- wet injection equipment;
- disposable and non-disposable RPE, including storage.

Enclosures

316 Where an enclosure is being used to comply with regulation 16, employers should make sure that:

- it is properly maintained;
- a thorough visual inspection and check on the integrity of the enclosure, airlocks and ducting from air extraction equipment is carried out at least at the beginning of each shift;
- any defects found during inspection and testing are repaired immediately;
- air extraction equipment is operated while work is being carried out, during breaks and for at least one hour after each shift;
- appropriate air monitoring outside the enclosure is carried out, eg in situations where the air exhausted from the enclosure is discharged into an occupied building because it is not reasonably practicable to discharge externally;
- viewing panels are maintained/cleaned regularly to ensure good visibility;
- CCTV equipment being used should be kept in good working order;
- appropriate barriers are maintained on open sites.

317 A record of inspections, checks and any repairs should be kept on site for inspection by the enforcing authority.

Hygiene facilities

318 Where specific hygiene facilities are provided, employers should make daily checks throughout the duration of the work to make sure showers, heating, lighting, extractor units, battery charging facilities and residual current devices are all working.

319 Keep a record of inspections and defects on site for inspection by the enforcing authority.

320 Showers should provide sufficient quantities of water at a reasonable temperature and pressure to allow thorough decontamination. Blocked shower rosettes and systems which result in alternate hot and cold water are not acceptable.

Vacuum cleaners

321 A class 'H' vacuum cleaner (BS 8520-3:2009) is required for licensable work with asbestos and can be used for non-licensable work. Where class H

ACOP 13

vacuum cleaners are used, employers should also make sure that the equipment is:

- inspected daily when in use to ensure that the equipment works effectively and provides adequate suction;
- inspected weekly when in use to ensure it is in good condition, it is not damaged and is working effectively;
- thoroughly tested and inspected every six months by a competent person.

322 A record of inspection, examination, maintenance and of any defects repaired must be kept on site for inspection by the enforcing authority.

323 During licensable work, the waste bag must be inspected regularly to see if it needs to be emptied. Inspection and changing should be done under controlled conditions to prevent spread of contamination (ie within the enclosure by workers wearing PPE, including RPE).

324 Where class H vacuum cleaners are used for non-licensable work, arrangements will need to be made to ensure that the waste bag is replaced (as necessary) under controlled circumstances.

Guidance 13

325 When used for non-licensable work, class H vacuum cleaners will generally need infrequent waste bag changing as the quantities of dust involved in cleaning will be small. Often the class H vacuum cleaners are hired and the supplier/hire company will replace the bags at the end of the hire period. Where waste bags need to be replaced during the work, the employer should make arrangements for the bags to be removed by an asbestos licence holder under controlled conditions.

ACOP 13

Air extraction equipment

326 All necessary air extraction equipment (including air movers and negative pressure units) should be:

- visually inspected daily when in use;
- thoroughly examined and tested every six months by a competent person to make sure it is working properly to its design.

327 This includes extraction units on hygiene facilities and relevant equipment in laboratories handling asbestos.

328 A record of inspection, examination, maintenance and of any defects repaired must be kept on site for inspection by the enforcing authority.

Wet injection equipment

329 All wet injection equipment should be:

- visually inspected daily when in use;
- thoroughly examined and tested every 12 months by a competent person to make sure it is working properly to its design specification.

330 A record of inspection, examination, maintenance and of any defects repaired must be kept on site for inspection by the enforcing authority.

ACOP 13

Respiratory protective equipment

Disposable RPE

331 Disposable RPE should always be:

- stored in a suitable safe and clean location before use;
- examined in accordance with the manufacturer's instructions before use (pre-use examination) to make sure it is not damaged and is in good working order;
- disposed of as asbestos waste after use.

332 Pre-use examination should include checks on the condition of the:

- straps;
- facepiece, including the seal and nosepiece;
- exhalation valve, if fitted.

333 A face-fit check must be done to make sure the mask fits properly.

334 A copy of the manufacturer's user instructions should be available to the wearer. This will give information on simple fit checks, such as those involving blocking filters and inhaling to create suction inside the mask so any leakage can be detected.

Non-disposable RPE

335 Effective protection from non-disposable RPE is dependent on maintaining the equipment in good condition and in working order, through sufficient cleaning and decontamination and by carrying out regular checks and examinations. There are three separate examinations which should be carried out:

- a 'pre-issue' examination which needs to be carried out by a competent person before the RPE is issued to a wearer;
- 'periodic examinations' by a competent person regularly to make sure the RPE is in efficient working order;
- a 'pre-use' examination, carried out by the wearer before the RPE is used.

336 All wearers of non-disposable RPE should have received sufficient training to be able to complete the necessary checks.

Pre-issue and thorough examination and test

337 A competent person should examine non-disposable RPE before it is issued to any wearer for the first time. In addition, non-disposable RPE should also be given a thorough examination and test by a competent person at periodic intervals (see paragraphs 335–336). The pre-issue examination and thorough examination and test should visually examine each component in detail to make sure it is in good condition, is not damaged, cracked, broken or perished and it is working properly. In particular it should check:

- the condition of the head harness and facepiece (including the face seal, visor and breathing hose if fitted);
- the condition of inhalation and exhalation valves (if fitted);
- the condition of any threaded connections, gaskets and seals to ensure they can be fastened securely;
- that filters, where fitted, are the right type, undamaged, are fitted correctly and within their shelf life;

ACOP 13

- the condition of the battery unit and its charge;
- the airflow rate.

338 The examinations and testing should also include any additional checks as specified in the manufacturer's instructions.

339 Where air-fed RPE is used, the following checks will be necessary as part of the thorough examination and test. Check:

- the compressed air supply tube, low pressure tube and breathing hose for damage, eg splits, holes, deformation etc;
- the connection of the compressed air supply tube to a belt or harness is robust and takes the weight of the tube;
- the pressure/flow regulator is in good condition and where designed, permits user adjustment;
- the low flow/pressure warning indicator, eg warning whistle, is functioning and has not been modified;
- both modes of operation, ie filtering and air fed, are functional and that the changeover connection/switch is working correctly.

The 'pre-use' examination by the wearer

340 This should follow the same checks as those listed in paragraph 332 but does not need to involve the equipment being disassembled. The RPE should also be checked by the wearer before and after it is used to make sure that it is free from contamination and has not been damaged. There should also be a fit check to ensure the mask is properly fitted by the wearer.

Frequency of tests

341 Thorough maintenance, examinations and, where appropriate, tests of non-disposable RPE should be carried out at least every month, or more frequently where the risks to health and the exposure conditions are more severe.

342 However, in situations where respirators are only occasionally used, the RPE should be examined and tested before it is next used and maintenance carried out as appropriate. The person responsible for managing the maintenance of the RPE should decide on suitable intervals between examinations, but this should not exceed three months for equipment in use. Emergency escape RPE should be examined and tested following the manufacturer's instructions.

Record keeping

343 A record of fit testing, inspection, examination, maintenance and any defects that are repaired must be kept available on site for five years for inspection by the enforcing authority.

Decontamination, cleaning and storage of non-disposable RPE

344 There are specific requirements for the decontamination, cleaning and storage of non-disposable RPE. The equipment needs to be:

- decontaminated, cleaned and dried after each use;
- disinfected whenever the equipment is being transferred from one wearer to another;
- stored in a suitable safe and clean location before use.

Regulation 14 Provision and cleaning of protective clothing

Summary

This regulation requires employers to provide employees with adequate personal protective clothing appropriate for the work they will be doing. It also sets out the requirement for proper cleaning, maintenance and storage of the clothing.

Regulation 14

(1) Every employer must provide adequate and suitable protective clothing for any employee employed by that employer who is exposed or is liable to be exposed to asbestos, unless no significant quantity of asbestos is liable to be deposited on the clothes of the employee while at work.

(2) The employer must ensure that protective clothing provided in pursuance of paragraph (1) is either disposed of as asbestos waste or adequately cleaned at suitable intervals.

(3) The cleaning required by paragraph (2) must be carried out either on the premises where the exposure to asbestos has occurred, where those premises are suitably equipped for such cleaning, or in a suitably equipped laundry.

(4) The employer must ensure that protective clothing which has been used and is to be removed from the premises referred to in paragraph (3) (whether for cleaning, further use or disposal) is packed, before being removed, in a suitable receptacle which must be labelled in accordance with the provisions of Schedule 2, as if it were a product containing asbestos or, in the case of protective clothing intended for disposal as waste, in accordance with regulation 24(3).

(5) Where, as a result of the failure or improper use of the protective clothing provided in pursuance of paragraph (1), a significant quantity of asbestos is deposited on the personal clothing of an employee, then for the purposes of paragraphs (2), (3) and (4) that personal clothing must be treated as if it were protective clothing provided in pursuance of paragraph (1).

ACOP 14

Suitability of protective clothing

345 As part of the assessment for work with asbestos, employers must decide whether or not protective clothing is required. They should start with the assumption that protective clothing will be needed, unless there is no potential for physical contamination and/or airborne exposures will be extremely slight and infrequent. For licensable work, exposure is liable to be significant and employers will always need to provide a full set of PPE.

346 Protective clothing must be suitable and include footwear, whenever employees are liable to be exposed to a significant amount of asbestos debris or fibres. It should be appropriate for the job and protect the parts of the body likely to be affected. To be suitable, depending on the circumstances, the protective clothing must:

- **fit the wearer;**
- **be loose enough to avoid straining and ripping the seams;**
- **be comfortable enough to allow for the effects of physical strain;**
- **be suitable for cold environments;**
- **prevent penetration by asbestos fibres;**

ACOP 14

- **be elasticated at the cuffs, ankles and on the hoods of overalls and designed to ensure a close fit at the wrists, ankles, face and neck;**
- **not have any pockets or other attachments which could attract and trap asbestos dust;**
- **be easy to decontaminate or dispose of.**

347 Where indicated by the risk assessment, disposable overalls with a hood and boots without laces will be required. Where disposable overalls are used, Type 5 (under BS EN ISO 13982-1:2004+A1:2010),[13] are suitable.

Guidance 14

348 Overall head coverings should be close-fitting and cover the parts of the head and neck not covered by the facepiece of the respirator. They should be connected to the main overall. The head straps of RPE should be worn under the head covering.

349 Wellington boots are preferable to any other form of footwear because they are easier to clean. Lace-up footwear will trap asbestos fibres between the laces and should not be worn.

350 Other risks should be considered, not just those created by asbestos. For example where methods involve using equipment with naked flames, the protective clothing should not be flammable. Based on the outcome of the assessment, further PPE may also be required, eg waterproof clothing for outdoor work, gloves for direct hand contact with ACMs.

351 Those that do the job are usually best placed to know what is involved and what problems exist. They should be consulted and involved in the selection and specification of the equipment, as there is a better likelihood of PPE being used effectively if it is accepted by each wearer.

ACOP 14

Removal of contaminated protective clothing

352 Protective clothing should be:

- **removed before taking off RPE;**
- **removed before leaving the work area for any reason (including for meal breaks, other breaks and at the end of the shift);**
- **cleaned before removal. For licensable work use a class 'H' (BS 8520-3:2009) vacuum cleaner fitted with suitable attachments. For non-licensable (including NNLW) work, wet wiping may be adequate, based on the outcome of the risk assessment.**

353 If the protective clothing is to be reused (eg in licensable work), it should be placed in a storage area specifically provided for that purpose (eg in the airlock). If it is not to be reused, it should be placed in a suitable waste bag. If the clothing is to be removed from the premises for cleaning or disposal, it should be sealed in a labelled, dust-tight bag.

354 If an enclosure is being used, and the main hygiene facilities are connected to the enclosure, then, after preliminary decontamination in the airlock, protective clothing, including footwear, should be removed in the dirty end of the hygiene facility.

355 If the main hygiene facilities are not connected to the enclosure, employers will need to provide additional overalls (of a different colour to those worn inside the enclosure) for employees to wear after preliminary decontamination has taken place in the airlock, to allow transfer to final

ACOP 14

decontamination at the main hygiene facilities. Separate footwear should also be provided for use between the airlock and the main hygiene facilities.

356 Following work in enclosures, employers should make sure that non-disposable clothing and towels for washing are collected from the airlock and hygiene facility as soon as they have been discarded.

Cleaning, maintenance and storage

357 Protective clothing and towels that cannot be disposed of must be effectively washed after every shift. If the employer does not have the facilities and expertise for laundering asbestos-contaminated clothing, the employer must send it to a specialist laundry. Asbestos-contaminated clothing going to a laundry should first be placed in dust-tight bags which are soluble in hot water and can be loaded, unopened, into a washing machine. Place inner bags inside a second bag, which is labelled and is strong enough to remain dust-tight during transport and handling. Dripping wet overalls and other types of PPE should not be put into soluble bags as they may cause the bags to partially dissolve during transport, which could result in dust release when the outer bags are removed.

358 In most cases employers should treat disposable overalls as asbestos waste and dispose of them properly after every shift. Disposal after a single use may not be necessary for overalls used for occasional sampling, where there is a low risk of contamination.

359 At the end of the working period, employers must make sure that the bagged, contaminated protective clothing is:

- placed in a specific storage area; or
- disposed of as asbestos waste (especially disposable overalls which should be disposed of after every shift); or
- prepared for dispatch to a laundry.

360 Asbestos surveyors and those sampling materials for asbestos who do occasional sampling should use their judgement to determine whether or not their overalls may have been contaminated and need to be disposed of.

361 Contaminated protective clothing or materials must never be taken home. This includes contaminated towels, which should either be effectively washed after every shift or disposed of as contaminated waste.

362 Where the contaminated clothing is cleaned on the premises, or by a specialist laundry, the washer and drier used must be dedicated for this use to prevent the spread of any asbestos to other items of laundry. The room containing the washer and drier should have its own LEV, preferably an air mover fitted with high efficiency particulate arrest (HEPA) filtration. The employee loading the washer should be wearing suitable RPE for protection. The air from the drier should be discharged to the external atmosphere and never to an occupied workroom. Separate washing cycles should be used for heavily and lightly contaminated items.

363 The waste water from the washer should be filtered before going to drain. The filter should be treated as contaminated asbestos waste and disposed of as such when it is being replaced.

Regulation 15 Arrangements to deal with accidents, incidents and emergencies

Summary

This regulation requires employers to prepare procedures on what to do if there is an accidental, unplanned, uncontrolled release of asbestos fibre. Also, for licensable work, procedures must be planned, implemented and tested and warning systems should be in place. Details of this information must be given to the emergency services.

Regulation 15

(1) In the event of an accident, incident or emergency related to the unplanned release of asbestos at the workplace, the employer must ensure that—

(a) immediate steps are taken to—
(i) mitigate the effects of the event,
(ii) restore the situation to normal, and
(iii) inform any person who may be affected; and
(b) only those persons who are responsible for the carrying out of repairs and other necessary work are permitted in the affected area and that such persons are provided with—
(i) appropriate respiratory protective equipment and protective clothing, and
(ii) any necessary specialised safety equipment and plant,

which must be used until the situation is restored to normal.

(2) The remainder of this regulation applies only to licensable work with asbestos, and is without prejudice to the relevant provisions of the Management of Health and Safety at Work Regulations 1999.

(3) Subject to paragraph (5), in order to protect the health of an employer's employees from an accident, incident or emergency related to the use of asbestos in a work process or to the removal or repair of asbestos-containing materials at the workplace, the employer must ensure that—

(a) procedures, including the provision of relevant safety drills (which must be tested at regular intervals), have been prepared which can be put into effect when such an event occurs;
(b) information on emergency arrangements is available, including—
(i) details of relevant work hazards and hazard identification arrangements, and
(ii) specific hazards likely to arise at the time of an accident, incident or emergency, and
(c) suitable warning and other communication systems are established to enable an appropriate response, including remedial actions and rescue operations, to be made immediately when such an event occurs.

(4) The employer must ensure that information on the procedures, emergency arrangements and systems required by paragraph (3)(a) and (c) and the information required by paragraph (3)(b) is—

(a) made available to the relevant accident and emergency services to enable those services, whether internal or external to the workplace, to prepare their own response procedures and precautionary measures; and
(b) displayed at the workplace, if this is appropriate.

Regulation 15

(5) Paragraph (3) does not apply where-

(a) the results of the risk assessment show that, because of the quantity of asbestos present at the workplace, there is only a slight risk to the health of employees; and
(b) the measures taken by the employer to comply with the duty under regulation 11(1) are sufficient to control that risk.

ACOP 15

Uncontrolled release of asbestos

364 Employers must deal with all uncontrolled releases of asbestos into the workplace, quickly and appropriately. This applies to circumstances where asbestos is accidentally disturbed as a result of work or where asbestos is unintentionally released as a result of a failure of control measures, such as a leak from an enclosure.

365 The steps required to clean up such releases must be appropriate for the scale of the release and the potential for further release and spread of fibres.

366 The clean-up of any release that leads to potential exposures at or above the control limit or that are not sporadic and of low intensity, eg releases of asbestos lagging, loose fill, asbestos coatings (not textured coatings) or large-scale releases of AIB must be done by a licensed contractor.

Guidance 15

367 The clean-up of asbestos materials where the fibres are firmly linked in a matrix and that are essentially in good condition (ie mostly intact), eg asbestos cement, bitumen products, papers, textiles etc will probably not require a licensed contractor. Similarly, clean-up of small-scale release of AIB where it is in relatively discrete pieces and undamaged will probably not require a licensed contractor. The *Asbestos essentials* guidance contains details of suitable methods to follow when carrying out remedial clean-up and decontamination for a number of different asbestos materials.

ACOP 15

What to do if there is a release

368 In all cases, where there has been an uncontrolled release of asbestos materials into the workplace, employers should take steps to:

- **warn people who may be affected;**
- **exclude people from the area, who are not needed to deal with the release;**
- **identify the cause of the uncontrolled release;**
- **regain adequate control as soon as possible.**

369 In particular, employers must make sure that:

- **anyone in the work area affected who is not wearing PPE, including RPE, leaves that area immediately;**
- **arrangements are made to decontaminate anyone who is contaminated with dust and debris;**
- **any clothing or PPE is decontaminated or disposed of as contaminated waste;**
- **measures are taken to contain and reduce fibre release.**

370 For any employee who was not wearing adequate RPE or has been potentially exposed to asbestos fibres in an incident, a note that the exposure has occurred must be made on that employee's health record. If the employee does not have a health record, the note must be made on that employee's personal record.

ACOP 15

How to clean up after a release

371 If contamination is severe, a licensed contractor and analyst should be employed to thoroughly clean and check the area respectively. When cleaning up after a release, the employer must make sure that:

- the contaminated area is thoroughly cleaned of visible debris or dust that may have become contaminated by asbestos fibres;
- employees doing this work wear appropriate PPE, including RPE;
- employees use equipment and procedures appropriate for the task and have appropriate training and expertise;
- supervisors or managers make a careful check to make sure the work has been properly carried out;
- checks are made to make sure the area is thoroughly cleaned and safe for reoccupation. Air sampling should be done to confirm that the remedial measures taken have been effective;
- only those people essential for carrying out repairs and other necessary cleaning and maintenance work are allowed into the affected area (other than emergency services).

372 For non-licensable work, detailed guidance on the controls and procedures to be followed is available in *Asbestos essentials* and for licensable work in *The licensed contractors' guide*.

Accidents, incidents or emergencies involving licensable work

373 When carrying out any licensable work, employers must have prepared procedures to put into effect if there is an accident, incident or emergency, which could put people at risk, because asbestos is present.

374 Employers must also make sure information about emergency procedures is given to anyone who may be affected, including employees, others and the emergency services.

375 Employers should give employees enough information and instruction to properly protect themselves. This should include procedures for:

- raising the alarm;
- evacuation – and these drills should be tested and practised at regular intervals;
- communicating within and between work areas;
- contacting the emergency services;
- decontamination;
- clean-up.

Guidance 15

376 There needs to be sufficient resources and equipment on or near the site to enable swift, safe and effective clean-up.

377 Employers need to take account of the need to integrate procedures with general fire precautions for the workplace and plan for any additional risks, eg not hearing alarms because of RPE and the siting of enclosures. Employers must ensure employees are given enough information and instruction about the prepared procedures and arrangements if there is a fire. This should include:

- details of the nature of the fire alarms and/or systems;
- details of the communications systems, including how to raise the alarm;
- the location and means of escape to and from the area of the fire.

Guidance 15

378 Knowing the location and means of escape from an enclosure and the immediate surrounding area will be particularly important if the enclosure (or hygiene facility) is located in a part of the premises that is hard to reach, or if the escape is awkward or lengthy.

ACOP 15

Contacting the emergency services

379 For licensable work, there should be arrangements in place for contacting the emergency services if they are needed.

380 If there is an incident, accident or other emergency, employers must ensure sufficient information is available to the relevant accident and emergency services so they can prepare their own response procedures and precautionary measures. This includes:

- **communication arrangements on site;**
- **the type, condition and location of the asbestos;**
- **details of relevant hazards;**
- **arrangements for evacuation;**
- **decontamination procedures;**
- **the clean-up procedure.**

Guidance 15

381 For licensable work, pre-planned procedures, hazard information, drills, and special warning or communication systems will not be required if the quantity or the condition of the asbestos in the workplace presents only a slight risk to the health of employees.

Regulation 16 Duty to prevent or reduce the spread of asbestos

Summary

This regulation requires employers to prevent or reduce the spread of asbestos anywhere work is being carried out under their control.

Regulation 16

Every employer must prevent or, where this is not reasonably practicable, reduce to the lowest level reasonably practicable the spread of asbestos from any place where work under the employer's control is carried out.

ACOP 16

Preventing/reducing the spread of asbestos

382 Employers should select and use work methods that will reduce the disturbance and release of asbestos fragments and fibres to minimise the risk of spread, eg by removing items intact or whole and by using dust suppression techniques.

383 Inside the work area, ACMs must never be left loose or in a state where they can be trampled on or spread. All asbestos waste should be bagged or wrapped promptly after removal and the waste should be removed from the work area regularly.

Enclosures

384 For most licensable work with asbestos, it is likely that a full enclosure will be required, unless it is not reasonably practicable.

ACOP **16**

Enclosures for non-licensable work (including NNLW)

385 Full enclosures will not normally be required for non-licensable work with asbestos cement or other bonded materials or for some work outside or in remote areas. However, a partial enclosure should be used for removing external asbestos cement soffits. Information on enclosure types is provided in *The licensed contractors' guide* **and** *Asbestos Essentials.*

386 For other non-licensable work:

- **full enclosures must be used where there is risk of airborne or significant internal physical contamination (eg from debris);**
- **a full enclosure should be used for large-scale work (eg on textured coatings);**
- **a mini-enclosure may be used where work is minor;**
- **where a full enclosure is used for non-licensable work, air extraction airflow rates as specified for licensable work should be used.***

387 Where enclosures are not used, the employer's risk assessment should establish what will be required to make sure that, as far as is reasonably practicable:

- **the spread of asbestos is prevented;**
- **people not involved in the work are excluded from the area;**
- **the work area is totally cleaned after work is completed.**

Enclosures for licensable work

388 Employers should make sure that, as far as is reasonably practicable, the work area is completely enclosed, to contain any asbestos debris and airborne asbestos fibres, by:

- **erecting a purpose-made enclosure; or**
- **sealing the whole or part of the area where the work is to be carried out.**

389 For most licensable work, which is not external or in a remote area, a full fit-for-purpose enclosure will be required and should have:

- **a three-stage airlock with openings to allow entry and exit, designed to prevent or reduce spread of fibres out of the enclosure and that allows progressive personal decontamination on exit;**
- **a three-stage bag lock, with separate openings for removal of waste fitted with their own airlocks to reduce the spread of fibres out of the enclosure during removal of waste;**
- **airlocks of sufficient size (1 m x 1 m x 2 m minimum where space permits) to allow siting of decontamination equipment (eg footbath and bucket) and effective preliminary decontamination. There should be weighted flaps on each of the airlocks, located on the enclosure side;**
- **air extraction with high efficiency particulate arrest (HEPA) filtration and sufficient capacity to maintain a reduced air pressure in the enclosure, to a level that is below that outside the enclosure (negative pressure). The filtered air from the extraction unit should be discharged to the external atmosphere wherever reasonably practicable;**

* A mini-enclosure is a small enclosure or tent used to prevent the spread of contamination without air extraction. A partial enclosure is neither fully enclosed nor provided with air extraction. A full enclosure includes airlocks and negative pressure air extraction. Other than for activities such as preventing spread during large-scale removal of textured decorative coatings, most non-licensed work with asbestos will not require a full enclosure. Where a full enclosure is used, the airflow rate should not be less than 500 m^3/hr. The reference to licensable work rates at the end of paragraph 386 is a target flow rate which should be aimed for, in a manner that is proportionate to the risk.

ACOP 16

- an airflow of at least 8 air changes per hour for enclosures greater than 120 m^3 in size or an airflow of at least 1000 m^3 per hour for enclosures less than 120 m^3 in size. The enclosure size should include additional areas introduced during the asbestos removal, eg ceiling voids. The airflow provided by the negative pressure unit(s) should be based on the current performance of the equipment and not the original design specification;
- viewing panels and/or CCTV. The panels should allow as much of the work area as possible to be viewed and should be kept clean/ unobscured. Where viewing panels are impractical, eg in basements and upper floors, or do not cover all areas, use effective closed-circuit cameras.

390 If heating, ventilation and air-conditioning systems are present in the area where the enclosure is, they should be turned off and sealed for the duration of the work activity.

391 Erecting scaffolding when it is forseeable that the asbestos may be disturbed, and/or when the scaffold forms part of a live enclosure will be licensable work.

392 The ends of any scaffold tubes used in the enclosure or to access the asbestos work area must be sealed.

393 Where the structure of a building forms part of the enclosure, the employer should make sure of the effective sealing of areas such as:

- windows, doors, vents, grilles and apertures through which pipes and other services/facilities may allow air to pass through;
- surfaces which may not be easy to access or clean.

394 Enclosures should normally be designed and constructed so that asbestos materials are not disturbed until the enclosure is complete and under negative pressure. Where this is not possible (eg the area is already contaminated with asbestos debris):

- the asbestos debris must be cleaned up using methods to minimise fibre release before the enclosure is built;
- suitable PPE and RPE should be worn during pre-cleaning and any work likely to disturb asbestos during the building of enclosures.

395 Before starting work in the enclosure, a thorough visual inspection and smoke test must be conducted to check the enclosure's integrity. The filtered air extraction equipment must be tested to ensure it is achieving negative pressure and the required air change rate.

396 Where reasonably practicable, connect hygiene facilities for final personal decontamination directly to the enclosure airlock system or, if this cannot be done, they should be as close as is practicable and procedures for preliminary decontamination and transiting should be drawn up and followed.

397 Where reasonably practicable, the 'transit' and 'waste' routes should avoid occupied areas or, if that is not possible, the work should be carried out when the required transit areas are not occupied. If this cannot be done, conduct more rigorous preliminary decontamination and carry out more frequent inspection, checking and cleaning the routes.

ACOP **16**

398 Partial enclosures may be used for external removal of AIB soffits where full enclosures are not reasonably practicable.

399 Where enclosures are not used, additional controls, monitoring and inspection will be required to make sure that, so far as is reasonable practicable, the spread of asbestos is prevented and the work area is thoroughly cleaned.

Decontamination procedures for licensable work

Preliminary decontamination procedures

400 Employers must have clear procedures in place to prevent the spread of asbestos and the consequential potential risk of exposing others. These should cover employees leaving enclosures and removing waste from enclosures. Procedures should include making sure that:

- most contamination on employees is removed during the preliminary decontamination procedure within the enclosure and airlock;
- employees use a 'buddy' system to clean their PPE and RPE as thoroughly as possible whenever they leave the enclosure or work area;
- dedicated class H (BS 8520-3:2009) vacuum cleaning equipment is provided and fitted with suitable tools. It should be located inside the enclosure, immediately next to the airlocks;
- remaining residues are removed in the showers in the main hygiene facility;
- contaminated clothing is not taken into the shower area or the clean end of the hygiene facility.

401 Exits (for people or waste bags) should be designed and constructed to prevent, or if that is not possible, minimise, the escape of airborne fibres and allow 'negative-pressure' equipment to operate effectively.

402 In transiting situations, in the inner stage of the air lock, footwear should be cleaned in the footbath using a brush. Respirators (still worn and with the motor still running if using a powered-assisted model) should be wiped with wet cloths or sponges, using separate washing facilities to those provided for the footwear. All cloths, wipes and brushes should be treated as contaminated waste.

403 In the middle stage of the airlock, work overalls and boots should be removed and retained for next use. Transit overalls and footwear should be put on in the final compartment (outer stage) of the airlock.

404 Any plant or equipment contaminated with asbestos must be thoroughly decontaminated before it is removed from the enclosure for other use or disposal. If it cannot be decontaminated:

- the equipment must be cleaned so far as is reasonably practicable and wrapped or sealed to prevent release of asbestos;
- the outer surface of the wrapping or seal must be decontaminated before the plant/equipment is moved;
- exposure to and spread of asbestos must be prevented when unwrapping/unsealing plant and equipment.

Final decontamination procedures

405 RPE should not be removed until the wearer is in the shower and the respirator has been effectively wetted. In exceptional circumstances, eg

ACOP 16

where wearing full-facepiece-powered RPE during transiting introduces additional risks (eg lack of visibility or tripping), a suitable disposable respirator, or half-mask respirator can be worn between the enclosure and hygiene facilities. The exterior of RPE should be fully wiped clean before transiting. This procedure must be justified in the risk assessment. Also:

- thoroughly cleaned RPE can be taken out through the 'clean' area;
- disposable towels and equipment (eg RPE filters) should be treated as asbestos waste;
- contaminated equipment will need to be put into a sealable container and then taken out through the dirty area.

406 Once the removal of asbestos has started and until the area has been thoroughly cleaned ready for four-stage clearance, anyone (including analysts and supervisors) leaving the enclosure or working area should carry out preliminary and final decontamination (by properly using the main hygiene facilities, including the shower). The only exception to this is where there is an acute risk to workers' health or safety due to a medical emergency in the enclosure.

Removal of waste from full enclosures

407 Where practicable, remove waste bags from the enclosure via a separate bag lock. Waste bags should be placed in the inner stage of the bag lock, where they are decontaminated before being passed into the middle compartment of the bag lock.

408 In the middle stage of the bag lock, the waste bags should be placed into a second bag (ie an outer bag), sealed and the outer bag wiped down. The double-bagged waste should be placed in the outer stage of the bag lock.

409 The waste should be removed promptly from the outer stage of the bag lock by an 'outside worker' wearing appropriate PPE and RPE. The bags should be transferred directly to the waste skip or vehicle.

410 Under no circumstances should people exit the enclosure via the bag lock.

411 Where it is not practicable to have a separate bag lock system, the bag lock should be constructed from the inner or middle stage of the three-stage airlock which provides the entry/exit system for people. Waste bags should never be taken through the main hygiene facilities.

Waste removal outside the enclosure

412 All waste should be double bagged and the bags wiped down to remove surface contamination. Waste should be transported between the enclosure or work area and the skip or removal vehicle using the route likely to be safest during normal transit.

Licensable work in open sites

413 Where it is not reasonably practicable to enclose the work area:

- the work area should be marked by suitable warning notices and physical barriers appropriately placed;

ACOP 16

- **employers must assess the risks to workers and others nearby and if necessary, and as far as is reasonably practicable, the work should be done when other workers or members of the public are not nearby.**

414 Where it is not reasonably practicable to build a full enclosure, other containment and dust-suppression techniques should be used to prevent the spread of asbestos.

415 Where an enclosure is not used, the risk assessment should establish what will be required to ensure that, as far as is reasonably practicable, the spread of asbestos is prevented and the work area thoroughly cleaned.

Static sampling/air monitoring

416 Air monitoring to reduce risks from spread of asbestos is required to:

- **measure the background concentration of asbestos fibres in the work area during work, to check that the control measures are effective;**
- **measure background fibre levels outside the enclosure, particularly when the enclosure is in occupied premises. Check for fibre leaks around the perimeter of the enclosure and at the airlock and bag lock positions. Also conduct testing at the discharge location of the air extraction equipment, where it is sited internally;**
- **measure background fibre levels inside the enclosure when the asbestos work is complete, to ensure that it has been thoroughly cleaned and decontaminated before dismantling;**
- **carry out measurements for reassurance, eg after accidental release of asbestos fibres.**

Guidance 16

417 Further guidance on reducing asbestos spread during non-licensable work is provided in the *Asbestos essentials* task sheets.

418 Further guidance on reducing asbestos spread for licensable work is provided in *The licensed contractors' guide*.

Regulation 17 Cleanliness of premises and plant

Summary

This regulation requires employers to make sure that work areas, plant and equipment used for asbestos work are kept clean. It also requires the employer to make sure the area is thoroughly cleaned after work is finished.

Regulation 17

Every employer who undertakes work which exposes or is liable to expose any employees of that employer to asbestos must ensure that—

(a) the premises, or those parts of the premises where that work is carried out, and the plant used in connection with that work are kept in a clean state; and

(b) where such work has been completed, the premises, or those parts of the premises where the work was carried out, are thoroughly cleaned.

ACOP 17

419 To help cleaning and prevent the spread of asbestos, employers must choose work methods and equipment to prevent or reduce release of fibres and the build-up of asbestos waste on floors and surfaces in the working

ACOP 17

area. Wherever practicable, waste should be transferred directly into waste bags as workers remove the asbestos materials.

420 Employers must make sure that any asbestos dust and debris is cleaned up and removed regularly to prevent it accumulating (and drying out where wet removal techniques have been used), and at least at the end of each shift.

421 Procedures for cleaning premises and plant will need to take account of the need for cleaning following an accidental and uncontrolled release of asbestos.

Further measures

422 Procedures will need to be set up for cleaning:

- working areas, including transit and waste routes;
- plant and equipment;
- hygiene facilities.

423 Dustless methods of cleaning should always be used. This includes, wherever practicable, providing dedicated class H (BS 8520-3:2009) vacuum cleaning equipment fitted with suitable tools. Procedures for cleaning should make clear:

- the items and areas to be cleaned;
- how often they need to be cleaned;
- the cleaning methods, which should not create dust;
- any special precautions which need to be taken during cleaning, including the low-dust technique to be used, and the measures to take to reduce the spread of dust.

424 Dry manual brushing, sweeping or compressed air must not be used to remove asbestos dust.

Clean-up when work finishes

425 When work with asbestos comes to an end, the work area should be thoroughly cleaned before being handed over for reoccupation or for demolition. All visible traces of asbestos dust and debris should be removed and a thorough visual inspection carried out.

426 Where the work is licensable then the four-stage clearance procedure, which includes air sampling (see paragraph 438), should be carried out and a certificate for reoccupation issued.

427 Where licensable work is done out of doors (eg soffit removal), then clearance air sampling will not be needed. In this situation, the certificate for reoccupation should still be completed, but without stage 3 (air monitoring).

428 Clearance air sampling is not required for non-licensable work. However, a written statement of cleanliness will be required for the work area for some non-licensable work, eg after large-scale removal of textured coatings (see paragraphs 464–467).

Guidance 17

429 Surveyors and others taking samples are responsible for cleaning up any material they have disturbed, but are not responsible for cleaning up pre-existing dust and debris.

ACOP 17

Site clearance process for licensable work

430 Once asbestos removal is complete, the premises must be assessed to determine whether they are thoroughly clean and so fit to be returned to the owner/occupier. It is important that this includes the premises, any plant or equipment or parts of the premises where work with asbestos has taken place and the surrounding areas, which may have been contaminated. The areas requiring assessment for site clearance certification for reoccupation include the:

- enclosed area (including ceiling voids where AIB ceiling tiles have been removed and airlock and baglock) or the delineated work area where an enclosure has not been used;
- immediate surrounding area (for enclosures this will include the outside of walls and underneath polythene floors; for delineated areas this will include surfaces nearby either where asbestos may have been spread or where the pre-cleaning was not done properly);
- transit route if one has been used;
- waste route and area around the waste skip.

431 Those employing an organisation to carry out the four-stage clearance must ensure that the organisation is accredited to meet the relevant criteria in ISO 17020 and ISO 17025.[14]

432 The four-stage clearance should be carried out by the same organisation, and preferably by the same person, as this will help continuity and consistency and will avoid problems with interfaces at each stage of the process. The organisation carrying out the four-stage clearance should have the necessary independence to act completely impartially. If the analyst is contracted by the building owner/occupier, a copy of the clearance certificate should be made available to the asbestos removal company.

Guidance 17

433 Although not a legal requirement, it is desirable that the analyst is employed by the building owner or occupier for site clearance certification. This arrangement helps avoid any conflict of interest (perceived or real) there may be if the analyst is employed by the removal contractor. It also enables an independent party to be involved in resolving any problems during the clearance process. Also, it has a practical advantage that all results and certificates for reoccupation can also be issued directly to the person who has responsibility for the premises, as well as the contractor.

ACOP 17

Site clearance certification for reoccupation

Duties and roles

434 Employers have duties to:

- make sure other people are not exposed to asbestos;
- prevent the spread of asbestos;
- ensure that the premises or parts of premises where work with asbestos has taken place are thoroughly cleaned.

435 Compliance with these duties is helped by:

- pre-cleaning where necessary;
- choosing methods which reduce the amount of airborne asbestos and asbestos pieces to the lowest level reasonably practicable;
- controlling the waste produced;
- using enclosures to prevent spread of asbestos;

ACOP 17

- thorough cleaning of the work area and areas which may have become contaminated;
- visual inspection of the work area and areas which may have become contaminated;
- obtaining a clearance certificate for reoccupation of the area and a separate clearance certificate for the hygiene facility.

436 Site clearance certification for reoccupation should only be done when work has been completed and the employer of those who did the work has made sure the areas requiring clearance assessment have been thoroughly cleaned and allowed to dry. To do this, employers should follow the guidance in paragraph 459 on checking site condition, job completeness and carrying out a thorough visual inspection. Site clearance certification for reoccupation should normally be done in four successive stages, with the next stage only being started when the previous one has been finished.

Guidance 17

437 More complex jobs, eg where multi-enclosure clearance is required or where scaffolding remains on site, may involve an alteration to the clearance sequence. For example, common areas (such as the transit route and the area around the skip) on multi-enclosure sites would only be thoroughly cleaned when the job is finally finished.

ACOP 17

Four-stage process for licensable work

438 The four stages of site clearance certification for reoccupation are:

- Stage One – preliminary check of site condition and job completeness;
- Stage Two – a thorough visual inspection inside the enclosure/work area;
- Stage Three – clearance air monitoring – this is not required for external work;
- Stage Four – final assessment post-enclosure/work area dismantling.

439 Where practical, the areas to be assessed should be dry. So sealants (such as PVA) should not be used before any visual inspections or disturbed air tests. Where it is not practical for the area to be dry (eg where water occurs naturally) this fact should be recorded before the site clearance process begins.

440 Occasionally some surfaces or materials, eg concrete, require sealing before the disturbed air test, because they produce quantities of non-asbestos dust which would lead to an apparent failure in the air test. The use of sealants in this circumstance should only be done under the direction of the person carrying out the air test and the fact recorded before the clearance process begins.

441 In some circumstances, the floor of an enclosure may be covered with a 'sacrificial' layer of suitable floor material to prevent damage to the polythene underneath it, reduce the risk of slips and allow safe use of access equipment. Dust or debris may have penetrated between the sacrificial layer and the polythene, and it will be necessary to take up the covering (which may need to be disposed of as hazardous waste) before site clearance certification.

442 The extent of the immediate surrounding area will have to be established on an individual job basis. Areas near the work area where asbestos may have spread or that may not have been pre-cleaned before the start of the asbestos work should be included as part of the immediate surrounding area. These areas should be inspected as part of the four-stage clearance

ACOP 17

certification. Failing to do this may lead to risk of exposure during future work in the premises, because there is still asbestos contamination.

Stage One: Preliminary check of site condition and job completeness

443 The scope of clearance should be established. The plan of work kept at the work site should be checked and the extent of the clearance being sought agreed between the analyst and the asbestos removal contractor. The scope of the clearance should be recorded (eg on a diagram). A note should be made of any remaining asbestos outside the scope of the work.

444 The work area, enclosure, hygiene facilities, and controls should be intact, operating and clean, with all ACMs included in the scope of the work and non-essential equipment decontaminated and removed. The hygiene facilities should remain operable until a certificate for reoccupation has been issued. The work area, surrounding area, transit route, waste route, together with the area around the waste disposal storage and all sections of the hygiene facility must be free of obvious asbestos-containing waste and debris of any kind. If a viewing panel is fitted to the enclosure, this should be looked through so that a preliminary check can be made of the inside of the enclosure to see whether it contains any waste and debris. The result of these pre-inspections should be recorded.

Stage Two: Thorough visual inspection

445 A thorough visual inspection should then be carried out to make sure that all visible traces of asbestos and other dust and debris have been removed, as far as is reasonably practicable, from the enclosure (including airlocks) or work area. It is important to refer to the plan of work to check that all the asbestos due to be removed has been removed. To be thorough, this visual inspection should consist of the following three checks:

- the completeness of the removal of the ACM from the underlying surfaces and adjacent areas;
- the presence of any visible asbestos debris left inside the enclosure and airlocks or work area where there is no enclosure;
- the presence of fine settled dust on all surfaces, including high levels. Surfaces should be checked in hard-to-reach areas, eg high shelved areas, ceiling voids, door and window lintels etc.

Guidance 17

446 The thorough visual inspection is the most important part of the four-stage clearance process. Take enough time, care and attention to ensure all surfaces and areas in the work area are thoroughly inspected, in accordance with paragraph 445.

447 Suitable facilities should be made available to enable the inspection to be properly carried out, eg access platforms, so that higher levels of the enclosure can be inspected.

ACOP 17

Stage Three: Clearance air monitoring

448 Following successful completion of the thorough visual inspection, and before the enclosure is dismantled or the work area handed back to the owner/occupier, carry out air monitoring to check that the concentration of airborne fibres remaining in areas affected by the work is as low as is reasonably practicable. For enclosures, this is carried out with the enclosure

ACOP 17

intact and dry, but with the negative pressure unit switched off and the pre-filter capped and sealed.

449 The monitoring should be accompanied by activities which raise dust from the surfaces at least to a level consistent with normal use of the area and possible future work activities.

450 A record should be made of the type of disturbance method and the length of time it is carried out for. As many areas will subsequently be subjected to normal cleaning activities, air disturbance tests should be carried out, using a brush to raise potential dust. Any person carrying out air disturbance must wear appropriate PPE/RPE.

451 For work areas without enclosures, reassurance or background air testing is more appropriate than a disturbed air test.

452 In most cases it will be reasonably practicable to clean the working area thoroughly enough for the airborne fibre concentration in the enclosure/work area, after final cleaning, to be less than 0.01 f/cm^3. If measurements of 0.01 f/cm^3 or more are found, an investigation will need to be carried out to find out the cause. If it is found that the enclosure or work area has not been cleaned properly, it must be re-cleaned, visually inspected and remonitored.

453 The threshold of less than 0.01 f/cm3 should be taken only as a transient indication of site cleanliness, in conjunction with the thorough visual inspection, and not as an acceptable, permanent environmental level.

454 Air monitoring is not required for external work on asbestos, eg soffit work. However the other three stages of clearance should be followed and a certificate for reoccupation issued when these have been completed.

Guidance 17

455 Any investigation into failed airborne tests is likely to be carried out by both the contractor and the analyst between them.

456 See *The analysts' guide* for details of the method to use when undertaking clearance air sampling.

ACOP 17

Stage Four: Final assessment post-enclosure/work area dismantling

457 Once the enclosure or work area has passed visual inspection and clearance air monitoring, the enclosure or work area can be dismantled. Dedicated class H (BS 8520-3:2009) vacuum cleaning equipment fitted with suitable tools and suitable PPE, including RPE, should be available during dismantling, so any small amounts of asbestos debris which have become lodged behind the fabric of the enclosure or within folds in the polythene sheeting or on the floor underneath can be removed. Once the enclosure or work area has been dismantled, the area should again be visually inspected to make sure all debris has been removed.

458 Where there is evidence of dust and debris being released during dismantling of the enclosure, and this cannot be easily removed by vacuum, the site should be re-enclosed, recleaned, the visual inspection repeated and a disturbed air test carried out to make sure that the airborne asbestos fibre concentration is as low as is reasonably practicable, and in any case below the clearance indicator.

ACOP 17

Clearance for reoccupation certification

459 Taking into account the results of each of the four stages of the clearance process, a certificate for reoccupation should be issued when the area concerned is deemed to be clean and cleared and suitable for return to the occupier. The certificate should include details of the site address, the dates and a brief description of the work, the name of the contractor, details of the clearance action done under each stage and the specific areas and items checked, the results of each stage, and the signature of the person completing each stage.

Clearance testing of hygiene facilities

460 Once the certificate for reoccupation has been issued for the work area, a clearance test should be carried out on the hygiene facility before it is removed from the site. The facility should be visually inspected and air tested. There should be a thorough visual inspection of all sections (ie clean end, showers and dirty end). The unit, including the shower, should be dry before the inspection takes place. On successful completion of the visual examination, a disturbed air test should be performed in the shower and dirty end. Clearance testing should be performed by a competent person. A separate clearance certificate should be issued for the hygiene facility. This certificate should be issued to the licensed contractor upon completion of the test and should be kept with the facility.

Cleanliness and clearance of maintenance areas

461 For premises permanently set aside for the testing and maintenance of plant and equipment contaminated with asbestos, the measures set out in paragraph 423 should be followed to keep the area clean. There should be a periodic, thorough visual inspection and disturbed air test to confirm the level of cleanliness. When such an area is to be used for non-asbestos work, the area will need to be thoroughly cleaned, the clearance process carried out and a certificate of reoccupation issued beforehand.

Guidance 17

462 The thorough visual inspection and disturbed air test should be carried out regularly.

ACOP 17

Duties of those issuing clearance certificates

463 The person who issues the site clearance certificate for reoccupation or the clearance certificate for the hygiene facility does not have direct duties under the Regulations. However, people issuing these certificates should follow this guidance to comply with their duty under section 3 of the HSW Act to protect the health of people other than their employees. They should also consider the provision in section 36 of the HSW Act, which may apply if the work they do leads to others who do have duties under the Regulations to fail in those duties.

Non-licensable work with enclosures

464 For some large-scale non-licensable work with asbestos, a full enclosure may be required to prevent or reduce spread of asbestos, eg the removal of textured coatings.

465 Once the work in these enclosures is complete, the area should be thoroughly cleaned before it is returned to the occupier. All visible traces of dust and debris should be removed before the enclosure is dismantled. A thorough visual inspection should be carried out.

466 Clearance air monitoring is not required as part of the clearance procedures and an independently provided certificate for reoccupation is not needed. The occupier should be provided with a written statement stating

ACOP 17

that the area has been thoroughly cleaned and visually inspected to make sure that no visible traces of dust and debris remain and the area is suitable for reoccupation.

467 The statement should include:

- **the site address;**
- **the dates of the work;**
- **a brief description of the work;**
- **the name and address of the contractor;**
- **details of the specific areas and items visually checked;**
- **the name and signature of the person completing the inspection.**

Guidance 17

468 More information on clearance procedures for non-licensable work is given in *Asbestos essentials*.

Regulation 18 Designated areas

Summary

This regulation requires employers to make sure that areas where asbestos work is being carried out are separated, clearly marked, and restricted to those required to work in the area. It also requires the employer to provide suitable facilities for employees to eat and drink.

Regulation 18

(1) Every employer must ensure that any area in which work under the control of that employer is carried out is designated as—

(a) an asbestos area, subject to regulation 3(2), where any employee would be liable to be exposed to asbestos in that area; and
(b) a respirator zone where the risk assessment cannot clearly demonstrate that the control limit will not be exceeded.

(2) Asbestos areas and respirator zones must be clearly and separately demarcated and identified by notices indicating—

(a) that the area is an asbestos area or a respirator zone or both, as the case may be; and
(b) in the case of a respirator zone, that the exposure of an employee who enters it is liable to exceed the control limit and that respiratory protective equipment must be worn.

(3) The employer must not permit any employee, other than an employee who is required for work purposes to be in an area designated as an asbestos area or a respirator zone, to enter or remain in any such area and only employees who are so permitted shall enter or remain in such an area.

(4) Every employer must ensure that only competent employees—

(a) enter a respirator zone; and
(b) supervise any employees who enter a respirator zone,

and for the purposes of this paragraph, a competent employee means an employee who has received adequate information, instruction and training.

Regulation 18

(5) Every employer must ensure that—

(a) the employer's employees do not eat, drink or smoke in an area designated as an asbestos area or a respirator zone; and
(b) arrangements are made for such employees to eat or drink in some other place.

ACOP 18

469 All areas where there is asbestos work should be segregated and marked with suitable warning notices as asbestos areas, subject to the exemptions provided in regulation 3(2).

470 For licensable work, the work will, most likely, take place in an enclosure. However, where an enclosure is not used, employers should still give adequate consideration to prevent unprotected people from approaching the disturbance work in the asbestos area. It should still be designated an asbestos area and temporary barriers/roping off will be needed.

471 Any area where an employee may be exposed to asbestos to a level which may exceed the control limit must be designated as a respirator zone. Respirator zones, whether enclosed or not, must be segregated and marked up with suitable warning notices, including notices that RPE must be worn.

472 All licensable work with asbestos should be carried out in an area designated as a respirator zone and an asbestos area.

473 Where it is not necessary to segregate an asbestos area (due to the exemptions in regulation 3(2)) or to designate a respirator zone (because the control limit will not be exceeded, or is not liable to be exceeded), RPE will still be required unless it is not reasonably practicable.

Guidance 18

474 In cases where the work area is to be in an enclosure, place warning notices on the airlock and enclosure walls. In the absence of an enclosure, establish the work area using ropes or barriers at a suitable distance. Place warning notices at suitable locations around the work area and at the entrance.

475 In many situations, the asbestos area and respirator zones will be the same, eg for licensable work carried out in an enclosure. However, in certain circumstances, where work is being carried out in a respirator zone, it may be necessary to mark out a larger asbestos area outside the respirator zone to keep people away from the area.

ACOP 18

476 As an employer, ensure the following. For work in an asbestos area or respirator zone:

- **employees should only enter and remain in an asbestos area or respirator zone if they need to do so to carry out their work;**
- **employees must have received adequate information, instruction and training, so they are competent to enter a respirator zone and supervise any employees in their charge who enter a respirator zone;**
- **people undergoing training may enter a respirator zone, provided they are under the direct supervision of a competent person;**
- **employees entering a respirator zone must wear RPE.**

Guidance 18

477 Other essential personnel, such as analysts, tradespeople and the emergency services may enter a respirator zone, provided they have received adequate information, instruction and training and are wearing adequate RPE and PPE.

ACOP 18

478 Employers should make sure that food and drink is never consumed in an asbestos area or respirator zone. Employers should provide an area to eat and drink (for licensable work this should be located as close as is reasonably practicable to the hygiene facilities).

Regulation 19 Air monitoring

Summary

This regulation requires employers to arrange regular monitoring of airborne asbestos fibres and keep records of the results. It sets out how long the records should be kept and that they should be made available to employees or the regulator as required.

Regulation 19

(1) Subject to paragraph (2), every employer must monitor the exposure to asbestos of any employees employed by that employer by measurement of asbestos fibres present in the air—

(a) at regular intervals; and
(b) when a change occurs which may affect that exposure.

(2) Paragraph (1) does not apply where—

(a) the exposure of an employee is not liable to exceed the control limit; or
(b) the employer is able to demonstrate by another method of evaluation that the requirements of regulation 11(1) and (5) have been complied with.

(3) The employer must keep a suitable record of—

(a) monitoring carried out in accordance with paragraph (1); or
(b) where it is decided that monitoring is not required because paragraph 2(b) applies, the reason for that decision.

(4) The record required by paragraph (3), or a suitable summary thereof, must be kept—

(a) in a case where exposure is such that a health record is required to be kept under regulation 22 for at least 40 years; or
(b) in any other case, for at least 5 years,

from the date of the last entry made in it.

(5) In relation to the record required by paragraph (3), the employer must—

(a) on reasonable notice being given, allow an employee access to the personal monitoring record for that employee;
(b) provide the Executive with copies of such monitoring records as the Executive may require; and
(c) if that employer ceases to trade, notify the Executive without delay in writing and make available to the Executive all monitoring records kept by that employer.

ACOP 19

479 Personal sampling/air monitoring is required for a representative range of jobs and work methods to protect the health of employees. It should be done at regular intervals and when there is a change which may affect exposure.

ACOP 19

480 Where groups of employees are doing the same type of work in similar conditions, sampling can be carried out on a group basis. Individuals chosen for sampling in a group should be selected at random.

481 Personal sampling/air monitoring involves:

- **checking the concentrations of airborne asbestos employees are exposed to;**
- **confirming the adequacy of the controls and RPE, ie whether the RPE chosen provides the appropriate degree of protection where the level of asbestos fibres in air exceeds, or is liable to exceed, the control limit or a peak level measured over 10 minutes of 0.6 f/cm^3;**
- **establishing employee exposure records.**

Employee exposure records

482 All records of air monitoring should state the employer's business name and address, the site address where appropriate and the date of air monitoring, and should also include:

- **the type of work being done and, where relevant, its exact location;**
- **the type of sample, eg personal, static, clearance etc;**
- **the location of any static sampler;**
- **the date and time of sampling, the sample duration and the flow rate;**
- **if a personal sample, the employee's name, the task being performed and the category of RPE being worn;**
- **the length of time individuals are exposed;**
- **the measured fibre concentration;**
- **the fibre type, if known;**
- **the names and organisations of the sampler and analyst and the sampling and analysis method used.**

483 Records of air monitoring or a suitable summary must be kept for five years, except that, where employees are under medical surveillance, employers must keep the records or summary to supplement the health record for 40 years. Any summary of results should contain enough information about airborne fibre levels to allow individual average exposures for different types of work to be estimated as accurately as possible.

484 Employers should consult employees, safety representatives or representatives of employee safety when making arrangements for monitoring.

485 On reasonable notice being given, the records or summary of the airborne fibre monitoring must be made available to employees.

Guidance 19

486 The results from all personal monitoring carried out by the licensed asbestos removal contractor during the period of the licence should be collated and submitted to HSE as part of the licence renewal procedure.

ACOP 19

Sampling

487 Analysis must be undertaken using the 1997 World Health Organisation (WHO) recommended method.

Guidance 19

488 Further information and guidance on the sampling strategy, the methods for sampling and analysis and the reporting of results of air monitoring can be found in *The analysts' guide*.

Guidance 19

489 If employers decide air monitoring is no longer necessary, they should list the values and sources of information about the likely concentrations of asbestos in air for the activities and tasks being carried out. This should include previous air monitoring data on employees from the same or a similar type of removal job or relevant published data (for instance similar activities with similar material being disturbed, as given in *The licensed contractors' guide*).

Regulation 20 Standards for air testing and site clearance certification

Summary

This regulation requires employers performing their own air testing to do it in a way that meets the criteria as set out in ISO 17025. It also requires employers to make sure that any person they engage to perform asbestos air testing and site clearance is competent and accredited by the appropriate accreditation body.

Regulation 20

(1) In paragraph (4), "site clearance certificate for reoccupation" means a certificate issued to confirm that premises or parts of premises where work with asbestos has been carried out have been thoroughly cleaned upon completion of that work in accordance with regulation 17(b).

(2) Every employer who carries out any measurement of the concentration of asbestos fibres present in the air must ensure that criteria are met which are equivalent to those set out in the paragraphs of ISO 17025 which cover organisation, quality systems, control of records, personnel, accommodation and environmental conditions, test and calibration methods, method validation, equipment, handling of test and calibration items, and reporting results.

(3) Every employer who requests a person to carry out any measurement of the concentration of asbestos fibres present in the air must ensure that that person is accredited by an appropriate body as competent to perform work in compliance with ISO 17025.

(4) Every employer who requests a person to assess whether premises or parts of premises where work with asbestos has been carried out have been thoroughly cleaned upon completion of that work and are suitable for reoccupation such that a site clearance certificate for reoccupation can be issued must ensure that that person is accredited by an appropriate body as competent to perform work in compliance with the paragraphs of ISO 17020 and ISO 17025 which cover organisation, quality systems, control of records, personnel, accommodation and environmental conditions, test and calibration methods, method validation, equipment, handling of test and calibration items, and reporting results.

(5) Paragraphs (2) and (3) do not apply to work carried out in a laboratory for the purposes only of research.

ACOP 20

490 Those measuring asbestos fibres in air including, for the purposes of employee exposure monitoring, must take all reasonable steps to establish that they work in conformity with specified requirements in ISO 17025 through accreditation with a recognised accreditation body. Employers engaging such people must take all reasonable steps to establish that accreditation is currently valid.

ACOP 20

491 Employers performing their own measurements of asbestos fibres in air or of employee exposure should make sure that the work is performed and recorded and assessed by people with suitable training, supervision and quality control systems to enable the results to be equivalent in accuracy to those achieved under ISO 17025.

492 Similarly, those carrying out site clearance certification of work areas before handover for normal reoccupation must demonstrate that they conform with the specified requirements in ISO 17020 and ISO 17025 through accreditation with a recognised accreditation body.

Guidance 20

493 There are two aspects to the application of this regulation:

- circumstances where the occupier, as an employer, decides they have the competence to carry out air sampling in house without engaging a third party (regulation 20(2));
- where an occupier or employer engages a commercial analyst (regulation 20(3)(4)).

494 In the first case, the in-house work may be done without accreditation by an external body. But the effect of the regulation is to require that the measurement work is done to a standard equivalent to that used by accredited people, who must be used if an employer engages outside help.

495 The United Kingdom Accreditation Service (UKAS) is currently the sole recognised accreditation body in Great Britain. It is recommended that employers who contract analysts should actively search the UKAS website to identify accredited organisations to safeguard their interests. This will give an assurance of accreditation and an element of independence.

Regulation 21 Standards for analysis

Summary

This regulation requires employers performing their own analysis of material to check for asbestos in a way that meets the criteria set out in ISO 17025. It also requires employers to make sure any person they engage to perform analysis is accredited to ISO standard by the appropriate body.

Regulation 21

(1) Every employer who analyses a sample of any material to determine whether it contains asbestos must ensure that criteria equivalent to those set out in the paragraphs of ISO 17025 which cover organisation, quality systems, control of records, personnel, accommodation and environmental conditions, test and calibration methods, method validation, equipment, handling of test and calibration items, and reporting results are met.

(2) Every employer who requests a person to analyse a sample of any material taken to determine whether it contains asbestos must ensure that that person is accredited by an appropriate body as competent to perform work in compliance with ISO 17025.

(3) Paragraphs (1) and (2) do not apply to work carried out in a laboratory for the purposes only of research.

ACOP 21

496 Employers engaging people to analyse samples of materials to determine whether or not they contains asbestos must take reasonable steps

ACOP 21

to establish that they have a valid accreditation to ISO 17025 from a recognised accreditation body.

497 Employers performing their own analysis of samples should make sure that the work is performed, recorded and assessed by people equipped with suitable training, supervision and quality control systems, so the results are equivalent in accuracy to those achieved under ISO 17025.

Guidance 21

498 The United Kingdom Accreditation Service (UKAS) is currently the sole recognised accreditation body in Great Britain. It is recommended that employers who contract analysts should actively search the UKAS website to identify accredited organisations to safeguard their interests. This will give an assurance of accreditation and an element of independence.

Regulation 22 Health records and medical surveillance

Summary

This regulation requires employers to arrange appropriate medical examinations for any employees who carry out licensable work or NNLW. It also sets out what health records employers must keep and for how long.

Regulation 22

(1) For licensable work with asbestos every employer must ensure that—

(a) a health record is maintained and contains particulars approved by the Executive for all of that employer's employees who are exposed to asbestos; and
(b) that record, or a copy of that record is kept available in a suitable form for at least 40 years from the date of the last entry made in it; and
(c) each employee who is exposed to asbestos is under adequate medical surveillance by a relevant doctor.

(2) The medical surveillance required by paragraph (1)(c) must include—

(a) a medical examination not more than 2 years before the beginning of such exposure; and
(b) periodic medical examinations at intervals of at least once every 2 years or such shorter time as the relevant doctor may require while such exposure continues,

and each such medical examination must include a specific examination of the chest.

(3) For work with asbestos, which is not licensable work with asbestos, and is not exempted by regulation 3(2), the requirements in paragraphs (1)(a) to (c) apply and—

(a) a medical examination in accordance with paragraph (1)(c) and (2)(a) must take place on or before 30 April 2015;
(b) on or after 1 May 2015, a medical examination in accordance with paragraph (1)(c) and (2)(a) must take place not more than 3 years before the beginning of such exposure; and
(c) a periodic medical examination in accordance with paragraph (1)(c) and (2)(b) must take place at intervals of at least once every 3 years, or such

Regulation 22

shorter time as the relevant doctor may require while such exposure continues.

(4) Where an employee has been examined in accordance with paragraph (1)(c), the relevant doctor must issue a certificate to the employer and employee stating—

(a) that the employee has been so examined; and
(b) the date of the examination,

and the employer must keep that certificate, or a copy of that certificate for at least 4 years from the date on which it was issued.

(5) An employee to whom this regulation applies must, when required by that employee's employer and at the cost of that employer, attend during the employee's working hours such examination and undertake such tests as may be required for the purposes of paragraph (1)(c) and must furnish the relevant doctor with such information concerning that employee's health as the relevant doctor may reasonably require.

(6) Where, for the purpose of carrying out functions under these Regulations, a relevant doctor requires to inspect any record kept for the purposes of these Regulations, the employer must permit that doctor to do so.

(7) Where medical surveillance is carried out on the premises of the employer, the employer must ensure that suitable facilities are made available for the purpose.

(8) The employer must—

(a) on reasonable notice being given, allow an employee access to that employee's personal health record;
(b) provide the Executive with copies of such personal health records as the Executive may require; and
(c) if the employer ceases to trade notify the Executive without delay in writing and make available to the Executive all personal health records kept by that employer.

(9) Where, as a result of medical surveillance, an employee is found to have an identifiable disease or adverse health effect which is considered by a relevant doctor to be the result of exposure to asbestos at work, the employer of that employee must—

(a) ensure that a suitable person informs the employee accordingly and provides the employee with information and advice regarding further medical surveillance;
(b) review the risk assessment;
(c) review any measure taken to comply with regulation 11 taking into account any advice given by a relevant doctor or by the Executive;
(d) consider assigning the employee to alternative work where there is no risk of further exposure to asbestos, taking into account any advice given by a relevant doctor; and
(e) provide for a review of the health of every other employee who has been similarly exposed, including a medical examination (which must include a specific examination of the chest) where such an examination is recommended by a relevant doctor or by the Executive.

ACOP 22

499 Employers must keep a health record for any employee who carries out work notifiable as either licensable or NNLW. The information must be kept for 40 years in a safe place.

500 For licensable work and NNLW, the health record should be kept in a suitable form, which will allow each employee access, on request, to their own records. For licensable work it should contain the following:

- each employee's surname and first names, sex, date of birth, permanent address, post code and National Insurance number;
- a record of the types of work carried out involving asbestos, and, where relevant, its location, with start and end dates, with the average duration of exposure in hours per week, exposure levels and details of any RPE used;
- a record of any work with asbestos before current employment, if the employer has been informed;
- dates of the medical examinations under the Regulations;
- a recording and planning system which brings forward the next required examination date for each individual.

501 For NNLW, the employer must:

- enter the employees carrying out the work in a register or record, indicating the nature and duration of the activity and the exposure to which they have been subjected;
- have a recording and planning system which records the date of the last examination and brings forward the next required medical examination date for each individual.

Medical examinations for licensable work

502 Anyone who carries out licensable work must have been medically examined in the past two years by a doctor individually appointed by HSE for that purpose (an 'appointed doctor').

503 For licensable work, employers should obtain certificates of examination for all employees, including those stating they have been examined in the past two years; appropriate authentication must be done with the earlier employer or the examining appointed doctor.

504 A medical examination should be repeated every two years (or within a shorter time if advised by a doctor), but only while the employee continues to do or expects to continue to do licensable work. The examination must be carried out by an HSE appointed doctor.

Medical examinations for NNLW

505 Employees who carry out any NNLW must have a medical examination on or before 30 April 2015. From 1 May 2015, anyone carrying out NNLW should have been medically examined under the Regulations in the past three years.

506 After the first medical, an examination should be repeated every three years (or a shorter time if advised by a doctor), but only while the employee continues to do or expects to continue to do NNLW. For NNLW, the examination does not have to be carried out by an HSE-appointed doctor, it may be carried out by a non-HSE-appointed doctor, such as a local general practitioner.

ACOP 22

Further information on medical examinations

507 Medical examinations for licensable work and NNLW should:

- **take place in the employee's normal working time. Employees should co-operate if they are sent for such an examination;**
- **be at the employer's expense, including travel, lost working time and the doctor's fee;**
- **trigger a review of all methods of work, risk assessments, and co-worker health if an employee is diagnosed with an asbestos-related condition. The affected worker may need further medical and managerial redeployment assessment if continuing in current tasks might endanger themselves or others.**

Guidance 22

Health records

508 Health records kept for the purposes of regulation 22 are not the same as the medically confidential examination record, kept by a doctor in line with medical practice. The health record kept by the employer only contains the information set out in paragraphs 500–501.

509 Because an asbestos-related disease may not be diagnosed until many years after exposure to asbestos occurs, health records should be kept for 40 years after the date of last entry or until the employee concerned reaches the age of 80, whichever is the longer period. The records should be kept even if the employee leaves the employer.

510 Employers may make their own arrangements for keeping the data, but records should be kept so they allow employers to form a view of the typical degree and duration of each employee's exposure to asbestos during the time they worked for the employer. It is acceptable to estimate exposures provided those estimates are informed, ie based on similar tasks on similar ACMs.

511 Employee representatives or elected safety representatives should be consulted on the arrangements for keeping the data.

512 Individual employees are entitled to see their health records on request. Doctors should also be given access to the records, where this is relevant.

513 There is guidance for doctors carrying out asbestos medicals in *Guidance for appointed doctors on the Control of Asbestos Regulations 2012: Medical surveillance for workers carrying out licensed work with asbestos*[15] and *Guidance for doctors on the Control of Asbestos Regulations 2012: Medical surveillance for workers carrying out non-licensed work with asbestos*.[16]

514 There is a searchable database of appointed doctors on the HSE website at www.hse.gov.uk/doctors/index.htm.

Certificates of examination

515 Certificates of examination should be issued to both employee and employer and indicate the date an examination was carried out under regulation 22. For new employees, the employer should verify that the employee has had an examination in the previous two years for licensable work and in the previous three years for NNLW (after 1 May 2015). If necessary, they need to confirm the validity of a certificate with the previous employer or examining doctor. Certificates should be kept on file by the employer for at least four years from the date of issue.

Guidance 22

Other health surveillance requirements

516 The medical examination under the Regulations is not an indication of general fitness to work, such as doing strenuous removal activities or removal in confined spaces. In addition to the medical examination required for work with asbestos, health surveillance may also be required under the Management of Health and Safety at Work Regulations 1999. In addition, if an employee is undertaking work in confined spaces to which the Confined Spaces Regulation 1997[17] apply, medical advice on an employee's suitability to do this kind of work may also be needed.

517 There is further guidance on health surveillance matters on the HSE website at www.hse.gov.uk/health-surveillance.

518 If an employer has concerns about the general fitness for work of an employee, they should consider formally arranging for a fitness-for-work examination to be carried out, in addition to the asbestos medical.

Regulation 23 Washing and changing facilities

Summary

This regulation requires employers to provide suitable and sufficient washing, changing and storage facilities for employees, and sets out the specific requirements for hygiene facilities for licensable work.

Regulation 23

(1) Every employer must ensure that the following are provided to any of that employer's employees who is exposed to asbestos—

- *(a) adequate washing and changing facilities;*
- *(b) where an employer is required to provide protective clothing, adequate facilities for the storage of—*
  - *(i) that protective clothing, and*
  - *(ii) personal clothing not worn during working hours; and*
- *(c) where an employer is required to provide respiratory protective equipment, adequate facilities for the storage of that equipment.*

(2) The facilities provided under paragraph (1) for the storage of—

- *(a) personal protective clothing;*
- *(b) personal clothing not worn during working hours; and*
- *(c) respiratory protective equipment,*

must be separate from each other.

ACOP 23

519 The type and extent of washing and changing facilities provided should be determined by the type and amount of exposure indicated by the risk assessment.

520 Suitable facilities should be provided, including:

- **toilet facilities;**
- **facilities for washing and changing for non-licensable work;**
- **full hygiene facilities for licensable work;**
- **an area to eat and drink (for licensable work these should be located as close as is reasonably practicable to the hygiene facilities).**

ACOP 23

Hygiene facilities for licensable work

521 For licensable work, suitable and sufficient hygiene facilities must be provided to enable employees working with asbestos to be able to clean and decontaminate themselves. This is to prevent the spread of asbestos and reduce the risk of exposure of others. Suitable hygiene facilities, whether purpose built on site or a transportable dedicated decontamination unit (DCU), must be provided on the site and be fully operational before any work (including ancillary work) starts.

522 The hygiene facilities will need to have separate changing rooms for dirty, contaminated work clothing and for clean or personal clothing – known as 'dirty' and 'clean' areas respectively. The showers should be located between the two changing rooms, so that it is necessary to pass through them when going from one changing area to the other. All doors between each room and those leading to the outside from the 'dirty end' should be self-closing and provide an airtight seal. The 'clean' and 'dirty' ends should be fitted with adequate seating and be large enough to change in.

523 Hygiene facilities also need to be designed so they can be cleaned easily and:

- be fitted with effective air extraction equipment which maintains a flow of air from the clean to the dirty areas. The extracted air must be discharged through a high efficiency particulate arrest (HEPA) filter;
- be adequately heated – any gas heater mounted inside the unit must be a room-sealed type; open-flue types must not be used. All gas appliances and fittings should be maintained in a safe condition by a competent person;
- be adequately lit (with suitable light switches at both the 'clean' and 'dirty' ends);
- have suitable internal vents so that air can pass through the unit;
- be big enough, including allowance for enough separate storage for personal clothing and protective clothing and equipment in the 'clean' end and enough suitable containers for contaminated clothing, towels, filters etc in the 'dirty' end and shower area;
- have showers with an adequate supply of clean running hot and cold or warm water, at a suitable pressure. Sufficient soap or gel, shampoo, nail brushes and individual dry towels must be provided for asbestos workers and for any other person who may need to use the facilities for decontamination;
- have shower areas big enough to allow thorough decontamination and have means to support the power pack of a full-face respirator while it is still required to be worn (the power pack support should be out of the direct line of the shower to avoid contact with water and prevent damage to the batteries);
- have all waste water filtered before it is discharged to the drains. All filters should be treated as asbestos waste;
- have a wall-mounted mirror in the clean end of the unit;
- have the electricity supply routed via a 30 mA residual current circuit-breaker fitted at the point of entry into the unit, and the unit must be effectively earthed when in use. The electrical fittings and installation must be suitable for use in the facility and maintained in a safe condition by a competent person;
- be sufficient for the number of people likely to need them;
- be maintained in a safe condition and kept clean as far as is reasonably practicable.

ACOP 23

524 Maintenance records for DCUs (or copies of them) should be kept on site. The hygiene facility should remain operational and not leave the site until the job is complete and the certificate of reoccupation has been issued.

Regulation 24 Storage, distribution and labelling of raw asbestos and asbestos waste

Summary

This regulation requires employers to make sure that raw asbestos and asbestos waste is properly packaged, labelled, stored and transported.

Regulation 24

(1) Every employer who undertakes work with asbestos must ensure that raw asbestos or waste which contains asbestos is not—

(a) stored;
(b) received into or despatched from any place of work; or
(c) distributed within any place of work, except in a totally enclosed distribution system,

unless it is in a sealed receptacle or, where more appropriate, sealed wrapping, clearly marked in accordance with paragraphs (2) and (3) showing that it contains asbestos.

(2) Raw asbestos must be labelled in accordance with the provisions of Schedule 2.

(3) Waste containing asbestos must be labelled—

(a) where the Carriage of Dangerous Goods and Use of Transportable Pressure Equipment Regulations 2009 apply, in accordance with those Regulations; and
(b) in any other case in accordance with the provisions of Schedule 2.

Guidance 24

Management of asbestos waste

525 Asbestos waste describes asbestos products or materials that are ready for disposal, including building materials, dust, rubble, disposable PPE, rags used for cleaning and used tools that cannot be properly decontaminated.

ACOP 24

526 When packing asbestos waste:

- **it should be securely sealed in suitable, labelled bags, wrapping or packaging as it is produced;**
- **any bags, wrapping or packaging used must be designed, constructed and maintained to make sure that no asbestos fibres can be released during handling or transport;**
- **for most waste, double plastic sacks are suitable, provided they will not split during normal use;**
- **stronger packages must be used if the waste contains sharp metal fragments or other materials that could puncture plastic sacks;**
- **any waste where the escape of hazardous quantities of respirable asbestos fibres can occur during carriage should be placed in UN-approved packaging. This is available in up to 2 tonnes capacity. (This does not apply to asbestos cement or textured decorative coatings.)**

ACOP 24

527 When filling bags:

- make sure that the inner bag is not overfilled, especially when the debris is wet, and each bag can be securely tied or sealed;
- exclude air from the bag as far as possible before sealing. Precautions will need to be taken as the exhaust air may be contaminated;
- where practicable, the sealed packaging should be cleaned before it is removed from the work area or enclosure.

528 If the asbestos waste is not to be disposed of immediately, the sealed bags and packages should be locked in a suitable and clearly marked storage area, ie a lockable skip.

Large asbestos waste items

529 Wherever practicable, large items of rigid ACM such as sheets of asbestos cement and textured coatings attached to a board should not be broken up or cut down for disposal in plastic sacks.

530 The intact rigid waste should be double wrapped in suitable polythene sheeting (1000 gauge or equivalent) or other suitable material and labelled accordingly.

531 If the asbestos waste is not to be disposed of immediately, the wrapped package should be placed in a suitable and clearly labelled sealed receptacle, such as a lockable skip or freight container.

Transporting asbestos waste

532 Bags, wrapping or packaging containing asbestos waste should be appropriately labelled and transported to a licensed disposal site. A list of disposal sites is available from local authorities.

533 Asbestos waste should be transported in an enclosed vehicle, skip or freight container.

534 A suitable receptacle should be used to transport the asbestos waste to make sure that the bags, wrapping and packaging cannot become damaged or open up and release asbestos material or asbestos fibres during transit.

535 Asbestos waste must be transported in accordance with the specific requirements of the Hazardous Waste Regulations in England and Wales[18] and the Special Waste Regulations in Scotland.[19]

Labelling asbestos waste

536 Asbestos waste must be labelled:

- in accordance with the Carriage of Dangerous Goods and Use of Transportable Pressure Equipment Regulations 2009[20] where those Regulations apply; or
- where those Regulations do not apply, in accordance with Schedule 2 of the Regulations.

Guidance 24

Sorting waste

537 A waste processing licence may be required from the relevant environment agency for some waste management activities such as sorting ACMs from other debris.

Regulation 25 Interpretation of prohibitions

Regulation 25

(1) In this Part—

"asbestos spraying" means the application by spraying of any material containing asbestos to form a continuous surface coating;

"extraction of asbestos" means the extraction by mining or otherwise of asbestos as the primary product of such extraction, but does not include extraction which produces asbestos as a by-product of the primary activity of extraction; and

"supply" means supply by way of sale, lease, hire, hire-purchase, loan, gift or exchange for a consideration other than money, whether (in all cases) as principal or as agent for another.

(2) Any prohibition imposed on any person by this Part applies only to acts done in the course of a trade, business or other undertaking (whether for profit or not) carried on by that person.

(3) Where in this Part it is stated that asbestos has intentionally been added to a product or is intentionally added, it will be presumed where—

(a) asbestos is present in any product; and
(b) asbestos is not a naturally occurring impurity of that product, or of any component or constituent of that product,

that the asbestos has intentionally been added or is intentionally added, as the case may be, subject to evidence to the contrary being adduced in any proceedings.

Regulation 26 Prohibitions of exposure to asbestos

Regulation 26

(1) A person must not undertake asbestos spraying or working procedures that involve using low-density (less than 1g/cm^3) insulating or soundproofing materials which contain asbestos.

(2) Every employer must ensure that no employees are exposed to asbestos during the extraction of asbestos.

(3) Every employer must ensure that no employees are exposed to asbestos during the manufacture of asbestos products or of products containing intentionally added asbestos.

Regulation 27 Labelling of products containing asbestos

Regulation 27

(1) Subject to paragraph (2), a person must not supply under an exemption granted pursuant to regulation 29 or regulation 30 a product which contains asbestos unless that product is labelled in accordance with the provisions of Schedule 2.

(2) Where a component of a product contains asbestos, in order to comply with this regulation that component must be labelled in accordance with the provisions of Schedule 2 except that where the size of that component makes it impossible for a label to be fixed to it, neither that component nor the product need be labelled.

Regulation 28 Additional provisions in the case of exceptions and exemptions

Regulation 28

(1) Where under an exemption granted pursuant to regulation 29 or regulation 30 asbestos is used in a work process or is produced by a work process, the employer must ensure that the quantity of asbestos and materials containing asbestos at the premises where the work is carried out is reduced to as low a level as is reasonably practicable.

(2) Subject to paragraph (3), where under an exemption granted pursuant to regulation 29 or regulation 30 a manufacturing process which gives rise to asbestos dust is carried out in a building, the employer must ensure that any part of the building in which the process is carried out is—

(a) so designed and constructed as to facilitate cleaning; and
(b) is equipped with an adequate and suitable vacuum cleaning system which must, where reasonably practicable, be a fixed system.

(3) Paragraph (2)(a) does not apply to a building in which, prior to 1st March 1988, there was carried out a process to which either—

(a) as then in force, regulation 13 of the Asbestos Regulations 1969 applied and the process was carried out in compliance with that regulation; or
(b) that regulation did not apply.

Regulation 29 Exemption certifications

Regulation 29

(1) Subject to paragraph (3), the Executive may, by a certificate in writing, exempt any person or class of persons or any product containing asbestos or class of such products from all or any of the requirements or prohibitions imposed by regulations 4, 8, 12, 13, 21 and 22(5) and (7) and any such exemption may be granted subject to conditions and to a limit of time and may be varied or revoked by a further certificate in writing at any time.

(2) Subject to paragraph (3), the Executive may exempt emergency services from all or any of the requirements or prohibitions imposed by regulations 7 and 9; and any such exemption may be granted subject to conditions and to a limit of time and may be varied or revoked by a further certificate in writing at any time.

(3) The Executive must not grant any exemption under paragraph (1) or (2) unless having regard to the circumstances of the case and in particular to-

(a) the conditions, if any, which it proposes to attach to the exemption; and
(b) any other requirements imposed by or under any enactments which apply to the case,

it is satisfied that the health or safety of persons who are likely to be affected by the exemption will not be prejudiced in consequence of it.

Regulation 30 Exemptions relating to the Ministry of Defence

Regulation 30

The Secretary of State for Defence may, in the interests of national security, exempt any person or class of persons from the prohibition imposed by Part 3 of these Regulations by a certificate in writing, and any such exemption may be granted subject to conditions and to a limit of time and may be varied or revoked by a further certificate in writing at any time.

Regulation 31 Extension outside Great Britain

Regulation 31

These Regulations apply to any work outside Great Britain to which sections 1 to 59 and 80 to 82 of the 1974 Act apply by virtue of the Health and Safety at Work etc. Act 1974 (Application Outside Great Britain) Order 2001 as they apply to work in Great Britain.

Regulation 32 Existing licences and exemption certificates

Regulation 32

(1) An existing licence granted by the Executive under regulation 8(2) of the Control of Asbestos Regulations 2006 shall—

(a) continue to have effect as if it had been granted under regulation 8(2) of these Regulations;
(b) be of the duration and subject to the conditions specified in it as if that duration and those conditions had been specified under regulation 8(3); and
(c) be liable to variation and revocation under regulation 8(4) and (5),

and any requirement in such a licence concerning notification or any exception to such a requirement has effect as a requirement for notification under regulation 9, or as an exception to such a requirement under regulation 3(2) of these Regulations.

(2) An existing exemption granted by the Executive under regulation 7(1) of the Asbestos (Licensing) Regulations 1983, regulation 8(1) of the Asbestos (Prohibitions) Regulations 1992, regulation 25(1) of the Control of Asbestos at Work Regulations 2002 or regulation 32 of the Control of Asbestos Regulations 2006 continues to have effect and be subject to any limitation of time or any conditions specified in it and liable to revocation as if it had been granted under regulation 29(1) or (2) of these Regulations.

(3) An existing exemption granted by the Secretary of State for Defence under regulation 8(3) of the Asbestos (Prohibitions) Regulations 1992 or regulation 33 of the Control of Asbestos Regulations 2006 continues to have effect and be subject to any limitation of time or any conditions specified in it and liable to revocation as if it had been granted under regulation 30 of these Regulations.

Regulation 33 Revocations and savings

Regulation 33

(1) The Control of Asbestos Regulations 2006 are revoked.

(2) The amendments listed in Schedule 3 will have effect.

(3) Any record or register required to be kept under the Regulations revoked either by paragraph (1), or by any of the Regulations revoked by regulation 36(1) of the Control of Asbestos Regulations 2006 or by regulation 27(1) of the Control of Asbestos at Work Regulations 2002 shall, notwithstanding that revocation, be kept in the same manner and for the same period as specified in those Regulations as if these Regulations had not been made, except that the Executive may approve the keeping of records at a place or in a form other than at the place where, or in the form in which, records were required to be kept under the Regulations so revoked.

Regulation 34 Defence

Regulation 34

(1) Subject to regulation 21 of the Management of Health and Safety at Work Regulations 1999, in any proceedings for an offence consisting of a contravention of Part 2 of these Regulations, it is a defence for any person to prove that all reasonable precautions were taken and all due diligence was exercised by that person to avoid the commission of that offence.

Regulation 35 Review

Regulation 35

(1) The Secretary of State must from time to time—

(a) carry out a review of regulations 1 to 34;
(b) set out the conclusions of the review in a report; and
(c) publish the report.

(2) In carrying out the review the Secretary of State must, so far as is reasonable, have regard to how Council Directive 2009/148/EC which repealed and replaced Council Directive 83/477/EEC as amended by Council Directive 91/382/EEC and Directive 2003/18/EC of the European Parliament and of the Council, on the protection of workers from the risks of exposure to asbestos at work (which is implemented by means of regulations 1 to 34), is implemented in other Member States.

(3) The report must in particular—

(a) set out the objectives intended to be achieved by the regulatory system established by those regulations;
(b) assess the extent to which those objectives are achieved; and
(c) assess whether those objectives remain appropriate and, if so, the extent to which they could be achieved with a system that imposes less regulation.

(4) The first report under this regulation must be published before the end of the period of five years beginning with the day on which regulations 1 to 34 come into force.

(5) Reports under this regulation are afterwards to be published at intervals not exceeding five years.

Schedule 1 Particulars to be included in a notification

Schedule 1

The following particulars are to be included in a notification made in accordance with regulation 9, namely—

- *(a)* *the name of the notifier and the address and telephone number of that notifier's usual place of business;*
- *(b)* *a brief description of-*
  - *(i)* *the location of the work site,*
  - *(ii)* *the type and quantities of asbestos to be used or handled,*
  - *(iii)* *the activities and processes involved,*
  - *(iv)* *the number of workers involved, and*
  - *(v)* *the measures taken to limit the exposure of employees to asbestos, and*
- *(c)* *the date of the commencement of the work and its expected duration.*

Schedule 2 Appendix 7 to Annex XVII of the REACH Regulation – special provisions on the labelling of articles containing asbestos. Regulations 14(4), 24(2) and (3) and 27

Schedule 2

1. (1) Subject to sub-paragraphs (2) and (3), the label to be used on—

(a) raw asbestos together with the labelling required under the Chemicals (Hazard Information and Packaging for Supply) Regulations 2009 and the Carriage of Dangerous Goods and Use of Transportable Pressure Equipment Regulations 2009;
(b) asbestos waste, when required to be so labelled by regulation 24(3); and
(c) products containing asbestos, including used protective clothing to which regulation 14(4) applies,

must be in the form and in the colours of the following diagram and must comply with the specifications set out in paragraphs 2 and 3.

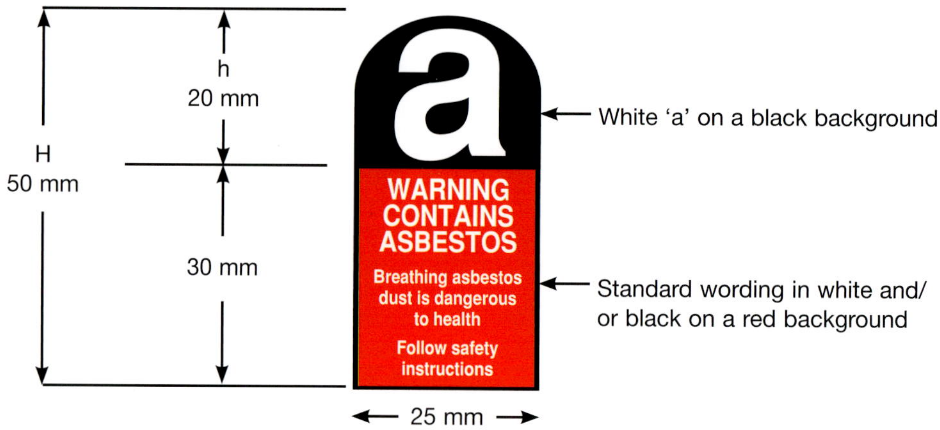

(2) In the case of a product containing crocidolite, the words "contains asbestos" shown in the diagram must be replaced by the words "contains crocidolite/blue asbestos".

(3) Where the label is printed directly onto a product, a single colour contrasting with the background colour may be used.

2. The dimensions in millimetres of the label referred to in paragraph 1 must be those shown on the diagram in that paragraph, except that larger measurements may be used, but in that case the dimension indicated as h on the diagram must be 40% of the dimension indicated as H.

3. The label must be clearly and indelibly printed so that the words in the lower half of the label can be easily read, and those words must be printed in black or white.

Schedule 2

4. (1) Where a product containing asbestos may undergo processing or finishing it must bear a label containing safety instructions appropriate to the particular product and in particular the following instructions—

"operate if possible out of doors in a well-ventilated place";

"preferably use hand tools or low speed tools equipped, if necessary, with an appropriate dust extraction facility. If high speed tools are used, they should always be so equipped";

"if possible, dampen before cutting or drilling"; and

"dampen dust, place it in a properly closed receptacle and dispose of it safely".

(2) Additional safety information given on a label must not detract from or contradict the safety information given in accordance with sub-paragraph (1).

5. (1) Labelling of packaged and unpackaged products containing asbestos in accordance with the foregoing paragraphs must be effected by means of—

(a) an adhesive label firmly affixed to the product or its packaging;
(b) a tie-on label firmly attached to the product or its packaging; or
(c) direct printing onto the product or its packaging.

(2) Where, in the case of an unpackaged product containing asbestos, it is not reasonably practicable to comply with the provisions of sub-paragraph (1), the label must be printed on a suitable sheet accompanying the product.

(3) Labelling of raw asbestos and asbestos waste must be effected in accordance with sub-paragraph (1)(a) or (c).

(4) For the purposes of this Schedule but subject to sub-paragraph (5), a product supplied in loose plastic or other similar wrapping (including plastic and paper bags) but no other packaging must be treated as being supplied in a package whether the product is placed in such wrapping at the time of its supply or was already so wrapped previously.

(5) No wrapping in which a product is placed at the time of its supply shall be regarded as packaging if any product contained in it is labelled in accordance with the requirements of this Schedule or any other packaging in which that product is contained is so labelled.

Schedule 3 Amendments

Schedule 3

Regulation 33(2)

Instruments amended	*References*	*Amendments to have effect*
The Personal Protective Equipment at Work Regulations 1992	*SI 1992/2966*	*In regulation 3(3)(c) for the words "the Control of Asbestos Regulations 2006" substitute "the Control of Asbestos Regulations 2012"*
The Health and Safety (Enforcing Authority) Regulations 1998	*SI 1998/494*	*In Schedule 2 paragraph 4A substitute the reference in paragraph 4(a)(iii) to "a physically segregated area does not include an area segregated only in order to prevent the escape of asbestos; and in this paragraph "asbestos" has the meaning assigned to it by regulation 2(1) of the Control of Asbestos Regulations 2012"*
The Provision and Use of Work Equipment Regulations 1998	*SI 1998/2306*	*In regulation 12(5)(b) for the words "the Control of Asbestos Regulations 2006" substitute "the Control of Asbestos Regulations 2012"*
The Control of Substances Hazardous to Health Regulations 2002	*SI 2002/2677*	*In regulation 5(1)(a)(iii) for the words "the Control of Asbestos Regulations 2006" substitute "the Control of Asbestos Regulations 2012"*
The Fur Farming (Compensation Scheme) (England) Order 2004	*SI 2004/1964*	*In Schedule 6 Part 6 paragraph 14(a)(i) and (ii) after the Control of Asbestos Regulations 2006" insert in each case from 6th April 2012, "the Control of Asbestos Regulations 2012"*

Schedule 3

Instruments amended	*References*	*Amendments to have effect*
The Health and Safety (Enforcing Authority for Railways and Other Guided Transport Systems) Regulations 2006	*SI 2006/557*	*In regulation 4(5) for the words "the Control of Asbestos Regulations 2006" substitute "the Control of Asbestos Regulations 2012"*
The Construction (Design and Management) Regulations 2007	*SI 2007/320*	*In regulation 17(1) for the words "the Control of Asbestos Regulations 2006" substitute "the Control of Asbestos Regulations 2012"*
The REACH Enforcement Regulations 2008	*SI 2008/2852*	*In Schedule 3 paragraph 2(b) for the words "the Control of Asbestos Regulations 2006" substitute "the Control of Asbestos Regulations 2012"*
The Merchant Shipping and Fishing Vessels (Health and Safety at Work)(Asbestos) Regulations 2010	*SI 2010/2984*	*In regulation 4(4) for the words "the Control of Asbestos Regulations 2006" substitute "the Control of Asbestos Regulations 2012"*

Appendix 1 Notice of Approval

By virtue of section 16(4) of the Health and Safety at Work etc Act 1974, and with the consent of the Secretary of State for Work and Pensions, the Health and Safety Executive has on 4 December 2013 approved the revised Code of Practice entitled *Managing and working with asbestos* (Second edition 2013, L143).

The revised Code of Practice gives practical guidance on safely controlling work with asbestos and asbestos-containing materials. It also gives practical guidance on the management of asbestos in non-domestic premises previously referenced in the Code of Practice L127 *The management of asbestos in non-domestic premises*.

By virtue of section 16(5) and with the consent of the Secretary of State for Work and Pensions under that paragraph, the Health and Safety Executive has withdrawn its approval of the Code of Practice entitled Work with materials containing asbestos and the Code of Practice The management of asbestos in non-domestic premises which came into effect on 20 October 2006 and which shall cease to have effect on 19 December 2013.

The Code of Practice comes into effect on 19 December 2013.

Signed

LOUISE STEVENS
Secretary to the Board of the Health and Safety Executive

19 December 2013

References

1 *Consulting workers on health and safety. Safety Representatives and Safety Committees Regulations 1977 (as amended) and Health and Safety (Consultation with Employees) Regulations 1996 (as amended). Approved Codes of Practice and guidance* L146 (Second edition) HSE Books 2012 ISBN 978 0 7176 6461 0 www.hse.gov.uk/pubns/books/l146.htm

2 *Health and Safety at Work etc Act 1974* (c.37) The Stationery Office 1974 ISBN 978 0 10 543774 1 www.legislation.gov.uk/ukpga/1974/37

3 *Asbestos: The analysts' guide for sampling, analysis and clearance procedures* HSG248 HSE Books 2005 ISBN 978 0 7176 2875 9 www.hse.gov.uk/pubns/books/hsg248.htm

4 BS 8520-3:2009 *Equipment used in the controlled removal of asbestos-containing materials. Operation, cleaning and maintenance of class H vacuum cleaners. Code of practice* British Standards Institution

5 *Asbestos essentials: A task manual for building, maintenance and allied trades on non-licensed asbestos work* HSG210 (Third edition) HSE Books 2012 ISBN 978 0 7176 6503 7 www.hse.gov.uk/pubns/books/hsg210.htm. Online versions of the *Asbestos essentials* sheets are available at www.hse.gov.uk/asbestos/essentials/index.htm

6 *Managing health and safety in construction. Construction (Design and Management) Regulations 2007. Approved Code of Practice* L144 HSE Books 2007 ISBN 978 0 7176 6223 4 www.hse.gov.uk/pubns/books/l144.htm

7 *The Management of Health and Safety at Work Regulations 1999* SI 1999/3242 The Stationery Office 1999 ISBN 978 9 99901784 8

8 BS EN ISO/IEC 17020:2012 *Conformity assessment. Requirements for the operation of various types of bodies performing inspection* British Standards Institution

9 *Asbestos: The licensed contractors' guide* HSG247 HSE Books 2006 ISBN 978 0 7176 2874 2 www.hse.gov.uk/pubns/books/hsg247.htm

10 *Asbestos licence assessment, amendment and revocation guide (ALAARG)* HSE50 HSE 2012 www.hse.gov.uk/pubns/hse50.htm

11 *Notification form* FOD ASB5 www.hse.gov.uk/forms/notification/fodasb5.pdf

12 *Notification of non-licensed work with asbestos* ASB NNLW1 https://extranet.hse.gov.uk/lfserver/external/asbnnlw1

13 BS EN ISO 13982-1:2004+A1:2010 *Protective clothing for use against solid particulates. Performance requirements for chemical protective clothing providing protection to the full body against airborne solid particulates (type 5 clothing)* British Standards Institution

14 BS EN ISO/IEC 17025:2005 *General requirements for the competence of testing and calibration laboratories* British Standards Institution

15 *Guidance for appointed doctors on the Control of Asbestos Regulations 2012: Medical surveillance for workers carrying out licensed work with asbestos* Medical Guidance Note MS31(rev1) HSE Books 2012 www.hse.gov.uk/pubns/ms31.htm

16 *Guidance for doctors on the Control of Asbestos Regulations 2012: Medical surveillance for workers carrying out non-licensed work with asbestos* Medical Guidance Note MS34 HSE Books 2012 www.hse.gov.uk/pubns/ms34.htm

17 *Safe work in confined spaces. Confined Spaces Regulations 1997. Approved Code of Practice, Regulations and guidance* L101 (Second edition) HSE Books 2009 ISBN 978 0 7176 6233 3 www.hse.gov.uk/pubns/books/l101.htm

18 *The Hazardous Waste (England and Wales) Regulations 2005* SI 2005/894 The Stationery Office 2005 ISBN 978 0 11 072685 4

19 *The Special Waste Amendment (Scotland) Regulations 2004* Scottish SI 2004/112 The Stationery Office 2004 ISBN 978 0 11 069030 8

20 *The Carriage of Dangerous Goods and Use of Transportable Pressure Equipment Regulations 2009* SI 2009/1348 The Stationery Office 2009 ISBN 978 0 11 148012 0

Further sources of advice

United Kingdom Accreditation Service (UKAS), 21–47 High Street, Feltham, Middlesex TW13 4UN www.UKAS.com

The Environment Agency (EA), National Customer Contact Centre, PO Box 544, Rotherham S60 1BY www.environment-agency.gov.uk

The Scottish Environment Protection Agency (SEPA), SEPA Corporate Office, Erskine Court, Castle Business Park, Stirling FK9 4TR www.sepa.org.uk

Natural Resources Wales (NRW)/Cyfoeth Naturiol Cymru, Tŷ Cambria, 29 Newport Road, Cardiff CF24 0TP www.naturalresourceswales.gov.uk

Further information

For information about health and safety, or to report inconsistencies or inaccuracies in this guidance, visit www.hse.gov.uk/. You can view HSE guidance online and order priced publications from the website. HSE priced publications are also available from bookshops.

British Standards can be obtained in PDF or hard copy formats from BSI: http://shop.bsigroup.com or by contacting BSI Customer Services for hard copies only Tel: 0845 086 9001 email: cservices@bsigroup.com.

The Stationery Office publications are available from The Stationery Office, PO Box 29, Norwich NR3 1GN Tel: 0870 600 5522 Fax: 0870 600 5533 email: customer.services@tso.co.uk Website: www.tsoshop.co.uk/. (They are also available from bookshops.) Statutory Instruments can be viewed free of charge at www.legislation.gov.uk, where you can also search for changes to legislation.

Published by the Health and Safety Executive 12/13